10 Minute Guide to

Applying to Grad School

by Ellen Lichtenstein
and Sharon McDonnell

alpha books

ARCO

A Division of Macmillan Publishing
A Simon & Schuster Macmillan Company
1633 Broadway, New York, NY 10019-6785

International Standard Book Number: 0-02-861192-6
Library of Congress Catalog Card Number: 96-085321

99 98 97 8 7 6 5 4 3 2 1

Interpretation of the printing code: the rightmost double-digit number is the year of the book's first printing; the rightmost single-digit number is the number of the book's printing. For example, a printing code of 97-1 shows that this copy of the book was printed during the first printing of the book in 1997.

Printed in the United States of America

Publisher: Theresa Murtha

Development Editor: Jennifer Perillo

Production Editor: Michael Thomas

Copy Editors: Chris Van Camp, Zackary Martin, Michael Thomas

Cover Designer: Dan Armstrong

Designer: Barbara Kordesh

Indexer: Bront Davis

Production Team: Angela Calvert, Kim Cofer, Tricia Flodder, Maureen Hanrahan, Beth Rago

Contents

Introduction

You're being pushed on all sides to go to graduate school—your parents, friends, co-workers, and even your employer say that getting an advanced degree will boost your career. And while you've always dreamed about the possibilities, you find the whole application process intimidating. All those things you've got to do—from taking the GREs and writing essays to getting recommendations from former professors—are headaches you would rather avoid. How can you study for tests, complete all the paperwork, get into a good program, come up with the money you need, and still start school next fall?

You know you need to:

- Follow a systematic application plan that helps you meet all deadlines
- Learn what factors are critical for getting into the program of your choice
- Understand how to write essays and personal statements that sell you to admission committees
- Find out if you are eligible for financial aid
- Get help in preparing for the Graduate Record Examination (GRE)

Because applying to graduate school involves a great deal of coordination and planning, you need the advice and straightforward information of this *10 Minute Guide*. Graduate school counseling, which is often difficult to obtain, is clearly presented in the proven *10 Minute Guide* no-frills format.

As a potential graduate school applicant, you probably do not have a lot of time to spare. You may still be in college studying for exams, or working a 40-hour week for a major corporation, or you may be at home raising a family. To learn all you need to know, you must make maximum use of your free time. The *10 Minute Guide to Applying to Grad School* will focus your research and teach you how to apply to graduate programs in easy-to-understand, 10-minute lessons.

WHAT IS A *10 MINUTE GUIDE*?

The *10 Minute Guide* series is designed to help you accomplish important goals by teaching you the essentials of a subject. Each book offers sound strategies for implementing actions and understanding new materials. In this book, through a series of lessons that take approximately 10 minutes each, you will learn commonsense graduate school application strategies including tips on getting recommendations, writing essays, obtaining financial aid, and taking the GRE.

USING THIS BOOK

You'll find 21 lessons inside this book; each concentrates on one area of the graduation school application process. You can read the book from beginning to end or just concentrate on the areas where you need help most.

CONVENTIONS USED IN THIS BOOK

The following icons will help you find your way around in the *10 Minute Guide to Applying to Grad School.*

> *tip* **Useful Tip** icons offer ideas that help you save time and avoid confusion.

Panic Button icons identify potential problem areas and how to solve them.

Plain English icons define new terms.

In addition to these icons, the text provides tables and illustrations to explain key points and simplify complex topics. Step-by-step instructions are highlighted to simplify complicated procedures.

By using this *10 Minute Guide*, you will have your own graduate school adviser behind you. Each lesson will get you closer and closer to securing admission to a graduate program and making your career plans a reality.

NOTE TO THE READER

It is beyond the scope of this book to cover professional school application strategies. Students can begin researching professional school by using many of the Arco professional test preparation books or school guides available in their school libraries or local bookstores.

FOR FURTHER REFERENCE

Look for these other Alpha and Arco books that will help you obtain your graduate school education:

- *The 10 Minute Guide to Paying for Grad School* by Ellen Lichtenstein

- *GRE SuperCourse* by Thomas H. Martinson
- *Preparation for the GRE—Graduate Record Examination* by Thomas H. Martinson (also available in book-disk version)
- *Graduate Record Examination in Psychology* by Sidney Raphael and Les Halpert
- *MAT: Miller Analogies Test* by William Bader, Daniel S. Burt, and Eve P. Steinberg
- *TOEFL SuperCourse* by Grace Qiu Zhong and Patricia Noble Sullivan

ACKNOWLEDGMENTS

A warm thank-you to all the education professionals who generously lent their time to help make this book a reality. Special thanks to Jennifer Caplan, Assistant Dean for Admissions and Financial Aid, Columbia University Graduate School of Arts & Sciences; Donald Taylor, Director, Graduate and Professional Admissions, Rutgers, The State University of New Jersey; Craig Pilant, Director of Admissions, Fordham University Graduate School of Arts & Sciences; William Crump, Graduate and International Admissions, Director, University of Memphis; and Mary Lou Balinskas, Director of Graduate Admissions, University of Connecticut at Storrs.

THE AUTHORS

Born and raised in New York City, Ellen Lichtenstein received her B.A. at City College of New York. During her publishing career, she has held senior editorial positions with two major publishers and has overseen the development and publication of hundreds of guidance, educational, and consumer reference books for both college and graduate school audiences. She is also the author of the *10 Minute Guide to Paying for Grad School* and the *10 Minute Guide to Building Your Vocabulary*.

Sharon McDonnell is a New York freelance writer whose articles are published in national and local magazines and newspapers. A former Senior Vice President at a top public relations agency and a former instructor of media writing workshops at New York University, she is also the author of *You're Hired! Secrets to Successful Job Interviews*.

LESSON 1

Deciding If Graduate Study Is Right for You

In this lesson you will learn how to decide if graduate school is right for you. You will also learn how to determine the right type of graduate study.

Why Go?

Figuring out your reasons for attending graduate school can help you select a school and a specific course of study. Your goal may be to:

- Teach at a college
- Obtain a professional license
- Increase your chances in the job market
- Increase your knowledge for its own sake
- Change your field
- Advance in your field
- Postpone the "real world" for a while

Choosing A Master's or Doctorate Degree

Figuring out your career goals can help in deciding which degree to pursue. Teaching or conducting research at the college level requires a doctorate. But in fields such as social work, library science, teaching at the high school or elementary level, engineering, or counseling, a master's is the only degree required for employment.

Master's Programs

Master's programs generally last two years. Depending on the field chosen, the degree can be an M.A. (arts), M.S. (science), M.S.W. (social work), M.F.A. (fine arts), M.L.S. (library science), M.P.H. (public health), and so on.

The master's degree program can be academic in nature, if your goal is to pursue research and scholarship, or it can be professionally oriented to prepare you to advance in occupations like social work, education, or journalism. Academic programs generally require a thesis—a 50- to 150-page paper that proves your knowledge of your field. Professional programs generally require fieldwork or extra classes instead of a thesis.

Financial aid is scant for master's programs.

The two types of master's degrees are:

- Terminal
- Awarded en route to the doctorate

Terminal, Not Fatal A terminal master's degree means that once you obtain your master's, you are not automatically accepted into a doctoral program, but must re-apply. This is because a master's offers sufficient training to advance in certain fields, such as social work. A doctorate is for students in these fields who plan to teach.

TABLE 1.1 STARTING SALARIES FOR SELECTED PROFESSIONS, MASTER'S VS. BACHELOR'S DEGREES, 1995

PROFESSION	DEGREE	STARTING SALARY
Accounting	Bachelor's	$27,900
	Master's	$31,500
Engineering	Bachelor's	$34,100
	Master's	$40,200
Social Work	Bachelor's	$17,500–$20,000
	Master's	$30,000

Source: Occupational Outlook Handbook, Bureau of Labor Statistics

DOCTORAL PROGRAMS

Doctoral programs generally last at least four years, often longer, and lead to a Ph.D. with the honorary title "doctor." You are trained to pursue independent research in your field. After one or two years attending classes and taking qualifying exams to prove your knowledge, you will start work on your doctoral dissertation, a lengthy paper that demonstrates independent research in your field.

Financial aid, in the form of teaching assistantships or research assistantships, is much more common in doctoral programs. The role of your advisor is much more important as well. Your advisor will work with you throughout your doctoral program and help you formulate your dissertation. You will often work for your advisor as a teaching assistant or research assistant.

Earning a Ph.D. is a rigorous process, and generally requires:

- Approval of your dissertation
- Knowledge of a foreign language
- Completion of classes, qualifying exams, and field training

The two methods to earn a doctorate are:

- Apply for a doctoral program
- Re-apply after earning a terminal master's

Some students pursue doctorates at the same graduate schools where they earned master's degrees. Others choose schools with a somewhat different focus to broaden their backgrounds.

Table 1.2 Median Time Spent in Doctoral Programs

Year	Length of Time in a Doctoral Program
1995	7.2 years
1984	6.9 years
1974	6.0 years

Source: National Research Council

Nondegree Programs

In nondegree, or nonmatriculated, programs, you attend classes, pay tuition, and do coursework, but do not earn a master's or doctorate.

Why a Nondegree Program?

You may choose a nondegree program for the following reasons:

You may be a returning student who wants to get reacquainted with the academic routine—and refresh your knowledge of the field—before pursuing a degree.

You may want to increase your knowledge—and gain a taste of graduate study—without committing to a degree program.

You may be uncertain if this is the field you should pursue.

Traditional vs. Nontraditional Students

Traditional students attend graduate school right after college. Nontraditional, or returning, students attend after being out of college at least 5 years—often 10–20 years or more—and after working and/or raising a family.

Nontraditional students are increasingly common in graduate schools, as many people opt to change careers or seek to improve their professional skills. Some schools have special advisors and facilities (such as child care centers) geared to older students to make the transition easier.

Table 1.3 shows that students aged 30 and older form the largest segment of our graduate school population.

TABLE 1.3 PERCENTAGE DISTRIBUTION OF GRADUATE STUDENTS BY AGE AND DEGREE PROGRAM

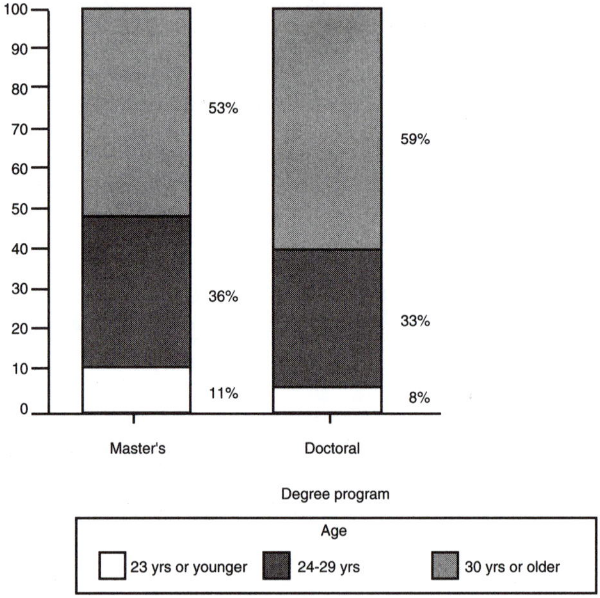

Source: Student Financing of Graduate and First-Professional Education, U.S. Department of Education, 1993

Don't Panic Don't let fears of the grind of term papers, library research, and all those fresh-looking faces in class scare you away. Many professors actually prefer nontraditional students, since they tend to be more mature and motivated to succeed. See lessons 5, 7, and 8 for advice about GRE (Graduate Record Examination) test scores, letters of recommendation, and other potential problem areas.

Full-time vs. Part-time Study

Because graduate school is much more intense than college—requiring heavy reading and independent research—try to attend full-time, if at all possible, particularly if you are in a doctoral program. Some programs do not even allow part-time study, which is far more common at the master's level. Of course, part-time study may be your only feasible option if you are working full-time and/or have a family.

Disadvantages of Part-Time Study

Part-time study presents several disadvantages:

- It takes a longer time to obtain a degree
- Financial aid is less available
- Part-time students often have less study time available
- Part-time students have to juggle competing pressures
- Part-time students are not viewed as seriously as full-time students
- Part-time students may receive different professors or may face different admissions standards than full-time students

Advantages of Part-Time Study

On the other hand, part-time study offers some advantages:

- Tuition is cheaper in the short run
- Part-time students take fewer classes per semester
- Part-time study may be easier to balance with work and family commitments

> **tip** **Advantage of Part-time Study** For full-time employees who want to go to graduate school, part-time study may be the best option. Going to school part-time allows you to hold on to your present job or continue working for your present company while gaining knowledge or skills for career advancement. In terms of finances, you can pay for your education through earnings or from employer tuition assistance programs. More and more graduate schools are offering part-time programs in specialized fields.

Joint Degree Programs

In joint degree, or dual degree, programs, you earn two different degrees at the same time. You apply to each program separately and meet the requirements of both. A joint degree program, such as social work and urban planning or law and business, generally takes less time to complete than pursuing the degrees consecutively.

Interdisciplinary Programs

Interdisciplinary programs, which involve classes and faculty from more than one department, are increasingly common and offer students a broader focus. You earn only one degree, however, in these programs, which may range from comparative literature to engineering combined with physics.

SUMMARY

In this lesson you learned how your goals help determine your choice of graduate study. You also learned the differences between master's vs. doctoral programs, degree vs. nondegree programs, traditional vs. nontraditional students, full-time vs. part-time study, and joint degree vs. interdisciplinary programs.

LESSON 2

Getting Information About Graduate School

In this lesson you will learn how to obtain information about graduate schools. You will also learn how to keep track of this information.

Where to Find Information

Information is like ammunition—the more you have, the better prepared you'll be in the application process. This lesson will discuss several sources of information about graduate school.

Books

Several directories list information about graduate programs, including addresses, telephone numbers, degrees granted, and the average GRE test scores of students accepted for admission. They can be found in libraries, bookstores, and your college placement office. These directories include:

- *Guide to American Graduate Schools* (Penguin)
- *Guide to Graduate and Professional Programs: An Overview* (Peterson's)
- *Index of Majors and Graduate Degrees* (College Board)
- Overviews of specific fields, e.g. humanities, physical sciences and mathematics, etc. (Peterson's)

Table 2.1 Most Popular Fields for Graduate Enrollment, Fall 1994

Field	Graduate Students Enrolled
Education	246,128
Business	168,084
Social Sciences	106,309

Source: Council of Graduate Schools

Professional Associations

Free or inexpensive information about programs and the career outlook for your specific field is offered by professional groups like the American Society for Engineering Education, American Psychological Association, and American College of Healthcare Executives. Check the *Encyclopedia of Associations*, found in libraries, to find the associations for your field and their addresses and telephone numbers.

Online Services

Free information on graduate schools can be found on the Internet and online services such as CompuServe and America Online.

Peterson's World Wide Web site (www.petersons.com) offers descriptions of graduate schools by name, program, and area. Many graduate schools and professional associations—some with career bulletin boards—also have their own Web sites.

Computer Software and CD-ROMs

Directories listing graduate programs with addresses, telephone numbers, etc., with the ability to search by specific field and area, are available from Peterson's and other publishers.

Rankings

U.S. News & World Report offers annual rankings of graduate schools, as does the book *The Gourman Report* (National Education Standards). These rankings will tell you which schools have the most prestigious programs in your field.

Graduate Schools

Call, e-mail, or write graduate schools for catalogs and applications. It's best to call the specific department or program you are interested in, instead of the central admissions office, because many programs have their own catalogs and applications.

tip

Read Between the Lines Catalogs are rich in information. But look beyond the glossy photos! Look for faculty members who specialize in your area, variety of classes in your area, and how many assistantships the program offers.

FACULTY

Professors at your college, or other professors you know, can be excellent sources of information about graduate schools and faculty, trends, and career outlook. Professors who are alumni can offer inside information on their alma maters as well.

Emeritus This honorary title, which you may see when you look up professors in faculty rosters or course catalogs, means a professor no longer teaches.

STUDENTS

Current students and alumni can also be excellent sources of candid advice about graduate schools, faculty (including the all-important choice of advisor), and career outlook. Ask graduate programs or local chapters of professional associations for names of students to contact in your area.

PROFESSIONAL JOURNALS

Read professional journals in the fields that interest you (for example, *American Sociological Review* or *Journal of Applied Physics*) to see which graduate schools are well-represented by professors writing articles.

VISITS

Visiting graduate schools that interest you can reveal a great deal about programs, student body, and faculty, as well as location, availability of affordable housing, etc.

INFORMATION WORKSHEET

Use the following worksheet to track the information you obtain from each graduate school. (See Lesson 3 for more on the factors to consider.)

SCHOOL: ______________________________

TELEPHONE NUMBER: ______________________________

ADDRESS: ______________________________

DEPARTMENT CONTACT NAME: ______________________________

NOTES ON PROGRAM: ______________________________

____

NOTES ON REPUTATION: ______________________________

____

NOTES ON FACULTY: ______________________________

____

NOTES ON TUITION\FEES COST: ______________________________

____

NOTES ON FINANCIAL AID: ______________________________

____

NOTES ON LOCATION: ______________________________

____

NOTES ON HOUSING, JOBS, SAFETY, CHILD CARE, ETC.: ______________________________

____

NOTES ON SIZE: ______________________________

NOTES ON RESEARCH FACILITIES: ______________________________

____

NOTES ON CAREER OUTLOOK FOR GRADUATES:

____

NOTES ON VISIT: ______________________________

____

STUDENT/ALUMNI CONTACT NAMES: ______________________________

FACULTY CONTACT NAMES: ______________________________

____

INTERVIEW REQUIRED: ______________________________

OTHER: ______________________________

FIGURE 2.1 Graduate school information worksheet.

SUMMARY

In this lesson you learned about many sources of information about graduate schools, and how to create a worksheet to track information received.

LESSON 3

Choosing a School and Program

In this lesson you will learn the factors to assess in choosing a graduate school and program. You will also learn how to assess your chances of getting accepted into a graduate school program.

Factors to Assess

Regardless of your reasons for attending graduate school—and whether your field is computer science, American Literature, or urban planning—you should choose a school and program based upon your own interests, goals, and preferences. Consider these factors:

Program

As you evaluate a particular graduate school program, consider the following questions:

- Does the program offer classes in your specialty?
- What are the academic prerequisites (certain classes, number of credits, minimum test scores or grade point average (GPA), internship, etc.)?

- What is the school of thought or orientation of the program?
- What is the foreign language requirement?
- Is there an option to the thesis?
- Is the program well-funded?

tip

Well-Funded or Poor Cousin? A small number of assistantships means the program is not well-funded. Some programs, which are well-funded, award assistantships to every student. Others award them competitively, or award more students smaller assistantships.

Reputation

As you evaluate the reputation of a particular graduate school program, consider the following questions:

- How is the program in your specialty ranked? Top-tier, second-tier, mediocre?
- What are employment opportunities like for graduates of the program?

Faculty

As you evaluate the faculty of a particular graduate school program, consider the following questions:

- Are there well-known professors in your specialty?
- Are well-known professors teaching and accessible to students?
- Who will make a good advisor?

RIGOR

As you evaluate the coursework of a particular graduate school program, consider the following questions:

- How much coursework is required?
- Are grades based upon exams at the semester's end or upon term papers you can research during the semester?

COST

As you evaluate the cost of a particular graduate school program, consider the following questions:

- What is the cost of tuition and fees? Are they calculated per credit or per semester?
- What is the availability of financial aid?
- What is the cost of living (housing, transportation, etc.) in the area?
- Do in-state residents pay a lower tuition than out-of-state residents?

FACILITIES

As you evaluate the facilities of a particular graduate school program, consider the following questions:

- What are the library, laboratory, and computer facilities like?
- Are the facilities open and available at convenient hours?

Location

As you evaluate the location of a particular graduate school, consider the following questions:

- Do you want to move or commute?
- Do you prefer a city, small town, suburban, or rural environment?
- What is on-campus or off-campus housing like?
- What are the job opportunities for you (and your spouse or partner, if applicable)?
- What are child care, entertainment, schools, and public safety like in the area?
- Do you prefer a certain climate?

Size

As you evaluate the size of a particular graduate school, consider the following question:

- Do you prefer a large school (bigger choice of classes, more diverse student body, more specialties) vs. a smaller school (more personal attention, smaller classes)?

Assess Your Chances of Getting In

To gauge if acceptance is likely, match your record against the records of the most recent entering class at graduate programs that interest you. Other ways you can assess your chances of acceptance include:

- Contact graduate programs or read a directory of graduate schools for average or median GPA and GRE test scores.

- Compare the program prerequisites listed in the catalog against your own. Certain classes, a specific major, or a certain number of credits may be required.

Programs vary widely in their acceptance rates. Some programs, like clinical psychology, are much more competitive than others; they receive hundreds of applications for just a few slots. Table 3.1 shows acceptance rates for various graduate programs.

TABLE 3.1 ACCEPTANCE RATES BY GRADUATE PROGRAM

PERCENT OF APPLICANTS ACCEPTED	PROGRAM
30%	Biological Sciences
32%	Social Sciences
45%	Engineering
65%	Education

Source: Council of Graduate Schools

tip **Diversity Desired** Women and minorities may be more desirable in certain programs where their numbers are fewer (such as engineering and computer science) even though their GPA and GRE scores may be lower.

RATING YOUR CHANCES

Use the following worksheet to compare your grades and test scores with those at graduate schools that interest you.

Rating Your Chances Worksheet

SCHOOL NAME: ____________________

REQUIRED OVERALL GPA: ____________________

MY OVERALL GPA: ____________________

REQUIRED GPA IN MAJOR: ____________________

MY GPA IN MAJOR: ____________________

REQUIRED GRE SCORE (GENERAL): ____________________

MY GRE SCORE: ____________________

REQUIRED GRE SCORE (SUBJECT): ____________________

MY GRE SCORE (SUBJECT): ____________________

PREREQUISITES: ____________________

AM I MISSING ANY?: ____________________

Figure 3.1 Acceptance requirements worksheet.

Pick the Schools Where You Will Apply

Armed with this valuable information, you can now pick a list of schools where you will apply. Of course, factors beyond grades and numbers—like a personal statement, letters of recommendation, and perhaps an interview—are also important in the admissions process. But for now, it's good to know if you're in the ballpark range of applicants a school typically accepts.

Pick one or two "safe schools" where your chances for admission look good because your GPA and GRE scores are higher than the school's numbers. These should be schools you would actually attend; don't waste your application fees on schools you have no intention of going to.

Pick two or three schools where your GPA and GRE scores closely match the school's numbers.

Last, pick one or two "ideal world" prestige schools you would love to attend—but at which you may not be accepted. You never know! Perhaps an outstanding personal statement will outweigh a weak spot in your application.

> *tip*
>
> **Save Money and Time** What's the point in applying to many schools, such as 15–20? Seven or eight should be your maximum, once you pick a "safe school" or two, "ideal world" school or two, and a few "middle-of-the-road" choices.

RANK THE SCHOOLS

Use the following worksheet to list the schools where you will apply.

List of Schools Worksheet

Real World ("Safe Schools")

1. ______________________________

2. ______________________________

Middle-of-the-Road

3. ______________________________

4. ______________________________

5. ______________________________

Ideal World

6. ______________________________

7. ______________________________

8. ______________________________

FIGURE 3.2 List of schools worksheet.

Summary

In this lesson you learned how to choose a graduate program suited to your needs and goals, how to assess your chances of getting in, and how to pick the list of schools where you will apply.

LESSON 4

Setting Up an Application Timetable

In this lesson you will learn how to plan a timetable to meet the deadlines for graduate school admission. You will also learn how to prepare a requirements checklist to track the process.

Start Early

How soon should you start the application process to graduate school? Sooner than you think. A year and a half before you start attending graduate school, at least, is generally a good time to begin planning the application process. This means the spring semester of your junior year if you are in college and plan to attend graduate school in the fall after graduation.

You should send in your application a year, or nearly a year, before you start attending graduate school.

Apply Earlier If You Want Financial Aid

Financial aid deadlines usually come earlier than regular admissions deadlines—generally in January or February of the year you plan to attend graduate school. If you want to be considered for aid, your entire application package must be sent in by the financial aid deadline.

> ! **Only Fall for Financial Aid** Although many schools admit students in the spring and summer as well as in the fall, some only consider students for financial aid for the fall semester.

Deadlines Are Important

Check admissions deadlines for each program carefully. They vary widely, even within the same school. Schools can be very strict about deadlines. Don't risk jeopardizing your application by mailing it late or incomplete.

Test dates are also important, and require planning ahead. For example, Graduate Record Examination (GRE) *print* tests (as opposed to the increasingly popular *computerized* version) are held only three times a year, in April, October, and December. It takes five to six weeks for applicants to receive their test scores, and another two weeks for graduate schools to receive the scores.

Therefore, an October or April test date—which permits an October re-take to aim for a higher score—is best if you plan to meet a financial aid deadline in January or February.

Computerized GRE tests offer more time flexibility, since they are offered year-round by appointment for at least two weeks out of every month, applicants receive their test scores immediately, and graduate schools receive the scores in two weeks.

tip

Earlier is Better Mail your application in plenty of time before the deadline. This way it can receive adequate attention and avoid being "lost" in the crush of applications around the deadline. If anything is missing from your application, you also have time to rectify the problem, instead of scrambling last-minute and possibly missing the deadline. Plus, it demonstrates your enthusiasm for the program.

DIFFERENT TYPES OF ADMISSIONS

Besides standard admissions, there are "rolling" and "early" admissions, where you will have to apply earlier. Check to see whether a program offers these options.

ROLLING ADMISSIONS

Many graduate schools (or certain programs in various schools) review applications periodically as soon as they are received, rather than waiting until the final deadline when all applications are evaluated as a whole. Check to find out if the programs you want to apply for have rolling admissions. If they do, apply as early as possible.

Advantage to rolling admissions:

- Applicants are notified immediately if they are accepted. This means you can be notified very early on, months before the regular admissions deadline.

Disadvantage to rolling admissions:

- All the spots may be taken if you dally until the deadline to apply—even if your application is spectacular—because applicants are being accepted all along.

Early Admissions

At some schools, you can apply a few months earlier than the regular admissions deadline, and be notified a month or two later. This is intended for applicants who are resolute about attending a certain school.

Advantages to early admissions:

- Applicants are notified soon after they apply, and avoid a long "waiting game."
- Applicants save money and time by not having to apply to many schools.

Disadvantages to early admissions:

- It's compulsory—intended for students who apply to *one* program, and, if accepted, go.
- Applicants may find a more ideal program later.

Timetable for Applying to Graduate School

The following timetable will help you organize your graduate school application plan.

Year and a Half Before Attendance

- Research graduate schools and specific programs in your field through books, online services, talking to faculty (if you are in college), and talking to graduate students.
- Narrow down the list of graduate schools and programs you are interested in by assessing factors like quality, size, cost, location, etc.

- Request catalogs and application materials.
- Talk to graduate schools about admissions requirements and other questions.
- Register and prepare for tests like the GRE.
- Research national scholarships.

Year and Three Months Before Attendance

- Take tests like the print GRE.
- Check on application deadlines.
- Contact the college registrar to send transcripts to graduate schools.
- Request letters of recommendation.
- Write your personal statement.
- Visit graduate schools that interest you.

One Year Before Attendance

- Take the computerized GRE test, the print GRE test (if you haven't already done so), or the retake of the GRE test.
- Get letters of recommendation.
- Send thank-you notes to the writers of your recommendations.
- Mail your completed applications.
- Obtain and complete the Free Application for Federal Student Aid (FAFSA), used for all Federal and a great deal of state and school financial aid.

Six Months to One Year Before Attendance

- Check with all graduate schools before deadlines to verify that your applications, letters of recommendation, and transcripts have been received.

Six Months Before Attendance

- Official notification of acceptance is generally in March for the fall semester. (If you plan to attend in another semester, check with the graduate school to find out the notification date.)

> ! **Not Just Tax Day** Hundreds of schools adhere to a Council of Graduate Schools resolution which states that applicants are not required to accept any financial aid offers before April 15. This means that you can rescind your acceptance if you land a better offer. Schools cannot make offers after April 15. The exception is if you have a written release from an offer you previously accepted.

- Ask for re-consideration if you are rejected by a graduate school that is your top choice.
- Select a graduate school from those that have accepted you.
- Mail a deposit to the graduate school you will attend.
- Notify other graduate schools that have accepted you of your decision to attend another school.

Checklist of Requirements

Use this checklist for every graduate school you apply to in order to track the application process:

SCHOOL NAME: ______________________
SCHOOL TELEPHONE NUMBER: ______________________
SCHOOL ADDRESS: ______________________
DEPARTMENT CONTACT NAME: ______________________
CATALOG/APPLICATION REQUEST DATE: ______________________
CATALOG/APPLICATION RECEIPT DATE: ______________________
APPLICATION DEADLINE: ______________________
APPLICATION FEE: ______________________
ROLLING ADMISSIONS, STANDARD OR EARLY: ______________________
DATE APPLICATION MAILED: ______________________
FINANCIAL AID MATERIAL REQUEST DATE: ______________________
FINANCIAL AID MATERIAL RECEIPT DATE: ______________________
FINANCIAL AID DEADLINE: ______________________

LETTER OF RECOMMENDATION #1: ______________________
NAME: ______________________
TELEPHONE NUMBER: ______________________
DATE REQUESTED: ______________________
VERIFIED SENT: ______________________
DATE SCHOOL RECEIVED: ______________________

LETTER OF RECOMMENDATION #2: ______________________
NAME: ______________________
TELEPHONE NUMBER: ______________________
DATE REQUESTED: ______________________
VERIFIED SENT: ______________________
DATE SCHOOL RECEIVED: ______________________

LETTER OF RECOMMENDATION #3: ______________________
NAME: ______________________
TELEPHONE NUMBER: ______________________

DATE REQUESTED:____

VERIFIED SENT:____

DATE SCHOOL RECEIVED:__________________________________

GRE SCORES REQUEST DATE: ______________________________

DATE SCHOOL RECEIVED GRE SCORES:_____________________

PERSONAL STATEMENT DUE DATE:__________________________

PERSONAL STATEMENT COMPLETION DATE: ________________

FIGURE 4.1 Application requirements checklist.

SUMMARY

In this lesson you learned how to set up an applications timetable and admissions requirements checklist, and learned the difference between rolling admissions and early admissions.

LESSON 5

Understanding How Admissions Decisions Are Made

In this lesson you will learn the criteria for graduate school admission. You will also learn who makes the decision for admission.

Criteria for Admission to Graduate School

Different graduate schools (and different programs of study, even if they are at the same graduate school) vary greatly in their admissions requirements. Read the graduate school catalog—and brochure for the specific program you are interested in, if there is one—carefully to see if the program requires minimum or average test scores or grade point average, a certain number of letters of recommendation, a personal statement, and so on.

> *tip* **Check Out the Competition** Read the program requirements carefully. Sometimes certain programs are much more competitive than others at the same school.

Generally, the criteria schools consider are:

- Undergraduate grade point average
- Standardized test scores from the GRE (general test, possibly subject tests as well), and possibly the Miller Analogies Test
- Letters of recommendation
- Personal statement
- Research ability
- Standardized test scores from the TOEFL (Test of English as a Foreign Language) for international applicants

Certain programs (such as clinical psychology) may also require interviews. Arts programs (such as music, fine arts, film, and writing) also require samples of your work, such as:

- Auditions
- Portfolios
- Videotapes/audiotapes
- Articles, stories, or term papers

Because programs vary in the amount of weight they give different criteria, contact the departments at the schools that interest you to find out which criteria they consider most important. Talking to current or former students is also helpful.

tip

Stacking Up Ask graduate departments for average GPAs and GRE test scores of the most recent graduating class, to get an idea of how you'll stack up. Also ask for ratios of number of applications received vs. number accepted. You can also find these figures in graduate school directories in libraries, bookstores, and placement offices.

The following sections will explain more about some of the most important admissions criteria.

UNDERGRADUATE GPA

Your undergraduate GPA is important, no doubt about it, because it shows how you have performed in an academic setting. The GPA in your major and in your junior and senior years is considered most important. Other factors considered are:

- The level of difficulty of the courses you took
- The reputation of your undergraduate institution
- Your overall course load
- How recently you were an undergraduate

> **!** **Don't Go Overboard** If you believe your GPA was lower than it should have been due to family, health, or money problems and does not accurately reflect your ability, say so in a short letter attached to your application or in your personal statement. A sentence or two will suffice—you don't want to look like you're making excuses.

TEST SCORES

Most graduate schools require GRE General Test scores. In addition, some programs, such as psychology and the sciences, require GRE Subject Tests as well.

GRE GENERAL TEST

The GRE General Test evaluates your knowledge and skills in three areas:

- Verbal (vocabulary and reading comprehension)
- Quantitative (high school math)
- Analytical (reasoning)

GRE SUBJECT TESTS

The GRE Subject Tests evaluate your knowledge of a specific subject, and are available in numerous subject areas. Most consist of multiple-choice questions.

GRE Subject Tests are available for the following subjects:

- Biochemistry, Cell, and Molecular Biology
- Biology
- Chemistry
- Computer Science
- Economics
- Revised Education
- Engineering
- Geology
- History
- Literature in English
- Mathematics
- Revised Music
- Physics
- Political Science

- Psychology
- Sociology

Source: GRE Board

In contrast to GPAs, there is more variation in how important GRE test scores are regarded in admissions to different graduate programs. In some programs, GRE scores are very important. In others, they are not. In some programs, scores on the three sections of the general test are equally important. Not so for others.

> *tip* **Brush Up** Good news: while there's not much you can do to raise your college GPA, the GRE is a different story. Test preparation books, courses, and software can raise your score by increasing your knowledge and the speed with which you can work through the questions. Practice on free sample tests, available from test-preparation companies, or "used" tests, sold by the Educational Testing Service (ETS), under identical time conditions to see how you'll score.

See Lessons 15 through 21 for more information about preparing for the GRE.

Miller Analogies Test (MAT)

The Miller Analogies Test (MAT), which tests thinking skills through the use of analogies, is required by some programs in addition to, or instead of, the GRE. However, the MAT is rarely used anymore.

See Lesson 21 for more information about preparing for the MAT.

Test of English as a Foreign Language (TOEFL)

The Test of English as a Foreign Language (TOEFL) is required for international students, unless their native language is English. It is administered by the ETS at testing centers abroad.

See Lesson 21 for more information about preparing for the TOEFL.

Letters of Recommendation

Graduate schools generally require three letters of recommendation. Some require more, some less. Ideally, these should be from college professors in your major, who are familiar with—and can say good things about—your knowledge of the field and your ability to do advanced study.

Letters of recommendation are very important, because they are third-party endorsements that distinguish you as an individual from the numbers of your grades and test scores.

See Lessons 8 and 9 for more information about letters of recommendation.

Personal Statement

This is a first-person essay that shows graduate schools how you think, how you express yourself in writing, why you want to pursue graduate study, and how much experience you have in the field. The personal statement is your chance to shine—to speak for yourself and make a strong case for why you will be an asset to a graduate school.

> ! **Tipping the Scales** Although personal statements are dreaded by many applicants, an effective personal statement can actually outweigh weak spots in your application. It is the only aspect of your application over which you exert complete control at this point in time. So make the most of this opportunity—write it with care, check it, and write it again.

See Lesson 7 for more information about writing your personal statement.

RESEARCH ABILITY

Graduate study is much more rigorous than undergraduate work. Analytical thinking skills and the ability to do independent research with minimal guidance are prized. Your letters of recommendation and personal statement should demonstrate your potential to make a contribution in your field.

WHO MAKES THE ADMISSIONS DECISION?

Admissions committees from graduate programs in specific fields of study generally make the admissions decisions. The admissions committee in a department of psychology, mathematics, or biology, for example, can be composed of from one to a dozen people.

The department admissions committee then sends its decision to accept or reject an applicant to the central admissions office, which sends an official notice of acceptance or rejection.

At some schools, a central admissions office first makes sure an application is complete and meets minimum criteria before sending it to the appropriate graduate department.

Sometimes, a graduate department may request a waiver of minimum admissions requirements from the central admissions office, if it feels strongly about an applicant. Usually, such waivers are granted.

Advice for Nontraditional Applicants

What do you do if your GPA and GRE test scores are old since you graduated from college years ago? (The ETS does not report GRE scores more than five years old, except for scores from 1976–85.) Or if you never took the GRE?

- Take graduate classes to show your current academic ability, brush up on your knowledge of the field, and find potential recommendation writers (i.e., grad school faculty or staff).
- Retake the GRE.
- Take test preparation classes or other methods to prepare for the GRE.
- Call graduate programs to ask for advice on finding suitable recommendation writers and meeting program requirements.

Summary

In this lesson you learned which factors graduate schools xconsider, and the important role admissions committees in departments play in granting admission.

LESSON 6

Learning the Secrets of Successful Applications

In this lesson you will learn the do's and don'ts of the application process, which will greatly increase your chances of admission. You will also learn what to do if you are not accepted to a graduate school program.

Tips to Successful Applications

The following tips will help you prepare and write an impressive graduate school application.

Organizing Your Application

- Keep all materials and deadline dates for specific graduate schools in separate files. If you store catalogs, letters, deadline schedules, and applications in one big pile, you'll get confused.
- Contact graduate school staff if you have any questions that are not adequately addressed in the catalog. Telephone or e-mail contact is best, since regular mail is often slow.

- If you call a graduate school for more information, ask for the director or coordinator of graduate studies in the specific programs you are interested in. If they are unavailable, ask for whomever can address admissions questions. Ask at the central admissions office if graduate program staff are unavailable.
- Identify yourself when you call a graduate school. Be professional and courteous at all times.
- Don't let your parents call. Graduate schools want to feel that you, as an adult, are handling the application process yourself.
- Ask if the graduate school accepts electronic (online) applications. This can save paperwork and time if you are computer-savvy.
- Ask if you can apply to more than one program at the same graduate school. At some you can. If you do, note that each program requires a complete application.

Filling Out Your Application

- Follow instructions carefully. Note the deadlines, the number of pages or words for personal statements, the number of recommendations, the address to which applications for your program should be sent, and so on.
- Photocopy the application, and fill out the photocopy before filling out the actual application. That way, you can write a rough draft, making sure all the information fits. If it doesn't, you won't have to request a fresh application.
- Type or print your application in ink. Messiness, odd colors, pencil, and illegible handwriting are turn-offs.

A computer or typewriter is best for completing your personal statement; a typewriter is best for completing the application because it will allow you to align the paper to fit the spaces.

- Make sure your application is complete. Blanks are turn-offs. Don't leave out your name, address, schools attended, etc., just because you are enclosing a resume.
- Make sure your application reflects organization and discipline. This way, graduate programs can concentrate on its content, without being distracted by form, such as bad grammar, spelling, and other signs of carelessness.
- Be accurate on applications. List all schools attended and supply transcripts, even if you failed to obtain a degree. Applications can be rejected for untruths.
- Proofread your application. Allow more than one responsible person to proofread it as well, because writers are often too "close" to what they have written to detect errors.

Self-Managed Applications You are responsible for obtaining and enclosing recommendations and transcripts in self-managed applications, which are becoming increasingly common.

INCLUDING EXTRA MATERIALS WITH YOUR APPLICATION

- Make sure you include all enclosures required. If the application fee is missing, your application will be regarded as incomplete.

- Note if recommendations and transcripts should be enclosed or sent separately. Note if supporting materials, such as term papers, essays, or photographs, are required.
- Don't overload your application with extra material that isn't required. Graduate schools don't appreciate applicants who send extra recommendations, overlong personal statements, and so on.
- Photocopy your GRE scores receipt and enclose it with your application. Generally, GRE scores are sent to graduate schools two weeks after being sent to applicants.
- Ask that your undergraduate transcripts be sent to you at the same time they are sent to graduate schools. This way, you know when graduate schools receive these transcripts. The cost is generally $2–$5 each.
- Include your name and social security number on all loose sheets of paper. This prevents personal statements and other documents from being lost if they get separated from the rest of your application.
- Make sure all enclosures are in the correct envelopes. Don't risk sending a personal statement that lauds a graduate school to its competitor!

SENDING YOUR APPLICATION

- Photocopy your application once you have finished filling it out so you have an identical copy in case your application is lost. (It happens.)

- Send your application before the deadline. (If you are running last-minute, use certified or overnight mail to meet deadlines.)
- Don't call graduate schools the weeks before or after application deadlines. Telephone lines are jammed at these "peak times."
- If the application includes a reply card, return it. Graduate schools will return the reply card (which should be stamped and self-addressed) and tell you whether your application is complete or is missing some documents.
- Create your own reply card or letter if none is enclosed with the application. Make sure it is stamped and self-addressed.
- Verify that your envelope includes the correct postage. Your potential future is enclosed in that weighty package—don't risk letting it sit in the dead letter office.
- Contact graduate programs a few weeks after sending your application to make sure it has been received and is complete.

See Appendix A for a sample graduate school application for admission.

IF YOU ARE NOT ACCEPTED

Sometimes it's not over, even though your application is rejected. Contact the graduate program to ask the reason for the turn-down, and if you can do anything to strengthen your application. You will probably be asked to submit a written request. Some schools may agree to reconsider your application, and may admit you after all. Others will advise you to reapply in a future year or semester, once you have added to your application in some way.

Because common reasons for rejection are low GPAs, insufficient academic background, and/or bad recommendations, a graduate school may ask you to:

- Submit another letter of recommendation
- Submit your completed transcript from your senior year in college
- Submit missing materials
- Take nondegree classes in the department
- Rewrite your personal statement
- Gain relevant work, internship, or volunteer experience

Summary

In this lesson you learned tips to help you prepare successful applications, what to do if you are not accepted, and how to strengthen your chances for acceptance next time.

LESSON 7

Writing Your Personal Statement

In this lesson you will learn the do's and don'ts to creating a successful personal statement. You will also learn why graduate schools think personal statements are so important.

The Purpose of the Personal Statement

The personal statement (or "Statement of Reasons for Graduate Study," "Statement of Purpose," etc.) strikes fear in many applicants' hearts. Because they are unsure what admissions committees want to read, and how to write it, they often dash off a statement hastily—or spend so much time on it that they choke the life out of it. Both approaches are mistakes.

The goal of a personal statement is to show graduate schools how you think and how you write, and to offer a window into your soul. As a "sales pitch" that reveals the real person behind the facts and figures, your personal statement should convince schools that you will be a valuable asset to their graduate programs. Think of it as an interview on paper—but one in which you have total control and can express yourself without interruption.

Some schools require only a few paragraphs; others, several pages. Some ask a specific question, such as why you want to attend graduate school. Others are completely open-ended, resembling the dreaded "Tell me about yourself" of job interviews. While schools vary in how important they regard personal statements, a successful statement can outweigh weak spots in your application or help you win out over other applicants with equally outstanding qualifications.

A SELF EXAM

Before you write your statement, a thorough self-assessment is necessary. Prepare by asking yourself the following questions and writing the answers. Don't worry about editing, style, or length at this point—the important thing is to get your ideas flowing.

- What is distinctive or unique about your family background and experience?
- What are the formative events and influences that have shaped your life?
- What is the most important thing about you that graduate schools should know?
- Have you conquered any obstacles or hardships in your life?
- Why did you select your field of study?
- What aspects of your field of study interest you the most?
- What are the personality traits that make you well-suited to your field of study?
- What are the skills (analytical, numerical, written, musical, etc.) that make you well-suited to your field of study?

- How have you learned about your field (college, adult education classes, work, friends or relatives, reading, etc.)?
- What are your career goals?
- Why do you want to attend this particular graduate school?
- What have you learned from your work, internship, or volunteer experience?
- Why will you be a success in your field compared to other applicants?
- Are there weak spots or discrepancies in your application you would like to explain (low GPA, low test scores, semester or year withdrawals, length of time in college, etc.)?

PERSONAL STATEMENT DO'S

The following tips will help you prepare an impressive personal statement:

- Make it sparkle. Paint a lively and interesting word portrait of yourself and your goals so graduate schools will remember you. Imagine that you are an admissions committee member who spends many tedious hours reading hundreds of dull personal statements each year!
- Demonstrate motivation and passion for your field. Explain the factors that caused you to choose it. Perhaps you studied the subject in college, and you yearn to delve into a specific specialty. Or perhaps an inspiring work experience was responsible for your decision to pursue this field.

- Follow the instructions. Adhere to the length restrictions, answer the question asked, and meet any other requirements. There are no right or wrong answers. If the statement is open-ended, you are free to focus on whatever theme you wish.
- Address an obstacle or challenge (financial, family, physical handicap, learning disability, etc.) you have overcome head-on. For example, explain why coping with poverty, immigrating to the U.S. without knowing a word of English, or coping with a parent's drinking problem has made you a stronger and better person. Don't dwell on the past, but on why and how mastery of a hardship will affect your future.
- Demonstrate analytical thinking. Graduate school statements are expected to be more mature than college application essays. As an adult, write thoughtfully about how you will fit into your field and the world at large—not just how the field will fit into your life.
- Back up your points with evidence. "I'm a hard worker" or "I'm well-suited to a career in clinical psychology" won't convince anybody. Persuade by using illustrative anecdotes or details.
- Make your statement "personal." Let your personality shine through. Write a statement only you—not other people in your field—could write.
- Grab attention with your opening paragraph. A ho-hum beginning won't encourage others to read further. Don't let the autobiographical nature of a statement fool you into thinking you should follow chronological order in the Dickensian "I was born" vein.

- Sustain attention throughout. Focus on one solid theme instead of rambling on in a scattershot approach. Make sure your ideas read smoothly, clearly, and tersely.
- View your life as a story. Then tell it. Imagine a camera scanning your life and its high and low points to develop the objectivity necessary to write an effective statement.
- Re-read and edit your statement. It's a good idea to put your statement away for a few days after completing it. Then review it with a fresh eye. Prune your sentences carefully.
- Have someone who knows you proofread your statement. A trusted friend, adviser, or relative can see things in your essay you can't, because you're too close to it. Listen to advice, but use your own judgment in the end.

PERSONAL STATEMENT DON'TS

Avoid the following common pitfalls when you prepare your personal statement:

- Don't make your statement too long or short.
- Don't make your statement too boring.
- Don't make your statement overly detailed.
- Don't allow poor grammar or spelling.
- Don't lie or exaggerate.
- Don't make grandiose goals or claims.

- Don't display a lack of analytical ability.
- Don't list accomplishments, work experience, or extracurricular activities without explaining their significance.
- Don't display a lack of maturity.
- Don't include irrelevant information.
- Don't use a "cookie cutter" approach.
- Don't use an impersonal tone.
- Don't be messy.
- Don't handwrite your statement.
- Don't use clichés.
- Don't be "cutesy."
- Don't delve into controversial areas, such as political, religious, or unconventional beliefs.

See Appendix B for a sample personal statement form required by a graduate school.

SUMMARY

In this lesson you learned the questions to ask yourself in order to write a personal statement that reflects you. You also learned tips to follow and pitfalls to avoid.

LESSON 8

Learning About Letters of Recommendation

In this lesson you will learn how to select the writers of your letters of recommendation, and factors to consider if you are currently in college or out of school.

The Purpose of Letters of Recommendation

Letters of recommendation are a valuable part of your application, because they distinguish you as an individual from the crowd of applicants and from the "numbers" of your GPA and test scores.

The letters should express confidence in your abilities and your motivation to do graduate-level work, and should help convince the graduate school that you will be an asset to your field. A vague letter that conveys the sense that the writer does not know you well—or a letter that is merely a character reference—is meaningless.

Check the catalog carefully for the number of recommendations your program requires, and supply that number. Most graduate schools ask for three. If a minimum number is requested, supply no fewer than the minimum and no more than one or two above that number. Don't overload your application—members of graduate school admission committees have more than enough to read as it is.

Also check the catalog for the type of recommendation writers your program requires. College professors, particularly those in your major area, are usually preferred.

> *tip* **Stay in Control** You have more influence over your letters of recommendation than you think. Select your recommenders with care, and help them do their job well by giving them the information and time they need.

Whom to Ask for Recommendations

As you consider potential recommendation writers, the following individuals should be among your top choices:

- College professors in your major area
- College professors familiar with your thinking and writing skills
- Professionals who have supervised you in internships or in work related to your graduate field
- Employers

The following individuals should be among your second-level choices:

- Colleagues
- Graduate students in your field

Stars Need Not Apply A letter of recommendation from a celebrity or prestigious person who barely knows you—but perhaps knows a family member or is a casual acquaintance—will not impress. However, if a well-known person is familiar with your work and willing to write a reference that goes beyond a mere form letter, this is a different story.

QUALITIES RECOMMENDATION WRITERS SHOULD HAVE

Your ideal recommendation writers should:

- Have a positive opinion of you
- Know you well
- Be familiar with your field of study
- Possess good writing skills
- Have teaching experience with many students to compare you favorably with your peers

It's a good idea to draw up a list of potential recommendation writers and their pros and cons. Nobody will be perfect. Then, narrow it down to a "short list" according to the above criteria.

Don't ever choose a recommender who does not like you, no matter how prestigious or known to the admissions committee he or she is. You run the risk of getting a spiteful letter that may prevent you from entering the program of your dreams.

tip

Think Ahead If you are unsure whether you will attend graduate school a few years down the road after college, check to see if your college can open a credentials file for you. Some college placement offices can keep letters of recommendation on file until you are ready to use them, which saves you time and trouble tracking them down later.

Advice for the Nontraditional Student

If you are a nontraditional (returning) student who has been out of college a few (or many) years, it may not be easy to locate college professors for recommendations if you did not set up a credentials file. Your undergraduate professors may have left, died, or—hard to believe—may not remember you.

Contact the graduate programs that interest you about alternatives. You may be able to submit letters from employers instead. Or you may be advised to take graduate-level courses in a nondegree program and submit letters from the professors after completion. The graduate school may even waive the recommendations requirement.

But don't just assume nonfaculty recommendations will suffice, or omit letters from your application. Policies vary widely, so ask specific graduate programs what they prefer.

See Appendix C for a sample letter of evaluation form included in a graduate school application.

Summary

In this lesson you learned how to influence your letters of recommendation by choosing appropriate writers. You also learned what to do if finding recommenders is difficult because you are a nontraditional student.

Lesson 9

Asking for Recommendations

In this lesson you will learn how to ask for letters of recommendation. You will also learn how to facilitate the process to produce the best letters for you.

20 Tips to Asking for Recommendations

Now that you understand the importance of letters of recommendation and how to choose letter writers, you will get to the heart of the matter: how to ask for a letter of recommendation, and how to help the writer produce an effective letter on your behalf.

1. Ask if your potential recommendation writers feel they know you well enough to be comfortable writing a meaningful recommendation.
2. Be quick to sense reluctance. Don't force the issue—and run the risk of obtaining a bad recommendation, a hastily written, vague recommendation, or no recommendation at all, leaving you high and dry days before your deadline.

3. Have a "Plan B" if any of your potential writers are unwilling to write, or fall through at a later date. Be ready with back-up choices.

4. Ask for recommendations early in the application process. The later you ask, the more likely it is that recommendation writing may interfere with work and personal obligations the recommender may have. You can even alert a potential writer that you may ask for a recommendation at a later time, after he or she gets to know you and your work better.

5. Make an appointment to discuss the recommendation. Don't just shove the recommendation forms in front of the person's face, say thanks, and leave.

6. Discuss your strong and weak points during the appointment, and brief your letter writer on your goals for graduate study and background. This dialogue prepares the writer so he or she can write a powerful, persuasive letter that draws a clear picture of how you will be an asset to a graduate program.

7. Bring materials with you. Besides the recommendation forms, bring stamped, addressed envelopes (if the letter writer is to mail the letter directly to the graduate school) or unstamped envelopes (if you are to enclose the letter with your application). Also bring supporting materials to back up the letter with details. This means a term paper, resume, transcripts, and your personal statement (or an outline or draft, if you haven't finished it yet).

8. If the letter writer is not a faculty member, he or she may be unfamiliar with the recommendation process. Explain the length required and the issues to cover in the letter.

9. If the letter writer is not a faculty member, ask him or her to explain his or her credentials in the letter. Also ask the recommender to describe in what capacity he or she supervises you.

10. Don't tell the recommender what to write. Just lay the groundwork with your discussion and supporting materials.

11. Discuss the confidentiality of the recommendation. Waiving your right to read the recommendation generally weighs more heavily in your favor, as the letter writer is apt to write more freely knowing you will not read it. (Sign the waiver on the form to waive your right.) In fact, many recommendation writers may not want to write a letter unless it is confidential.

12. Most self-managed applications (in which recommendations are enclosed) ask the recommendation writer to sign his or her name over the sealed flap on the envelope. This is proof you haven't peeked since receiving the recommendation.

13. Remember, you are asking for a favor (a time-consuming one), not issuing a demand. Act honored and courteous.

14. Tell your recommenders why you have selected them. It may guide them toward stressing certain issues in your recommendation.

15. Give the writer any materials that refer to the deadline date and/or special requirements so he or she can refer to them. Some programs ask recommendation writers to fill out questionnaires or rate applicants on their

strong and weak points in addition to writing the letter. Some ask for the recommendation on official letterhead with title and signature; others supply the form on which the letter is to be written. Make sure your letter writer has all the necessary forms and instructions.

16. If the recommender is writing more than one letter, explain the differences each program may require.
17. Provide your telephone number and address so the letter writer can reach you with any questions. Answer these promptly and fully.
18. Call your writers a few weeks before your application deadline to ask if they have any questions. This serves as a mild reminder that the deadline is near. It also gives you time to enact "Plan B" if a recommender unexpectedly drops out.
19. Call the graduate departments a week or two before the deadline to verify that all your recommendations have been received. If not, call your writers so that the letters can be sent in time.
20. Send thank-you notes to your recommendation writers after you send your applications (or acceptances, if you are wary of counting your chickens before they are hatched!). Inform them of the school you have selected.

Summary

In this lesson you learned 20 tips to proper etiquette when asking for letters of recommendation.

LESSON 10

Preparing for Interviews

In this lesson you will learn how to prepare for interviews and auditions. You will also learn the types of questions to ask, as well as questions you may be asked.

The Purpose of the Interview

Interviews often inspire nameless dread among applicants. The best way to conquer the fear of the unknown is to make it known and familiar so that it loses its power.

As you prepare for an interview, do your homework: build your questions around the factors to consider in choosing a graduate program discussed in Lesson 3. Practice answers to questions staff may ask you, which are generally the same topics as those addressed in personal statements.

Remember, an interview is a two-way process between you and the department—you both stand to learn from the experience. Some graduate programs ask certain applicants to come in for interviews after reviewing their applications. In programs like clinical psychology, which require interpersonal skills, an interview is usually required of all applicants. In other programs, you are welcome to request an interview. Some schools may offer to pay your transportation expenses; others leave you on your own.

TYPES OF QUESTIONS TO ASK

Here are some questions you can ask during your interview:

- What is the level of interaction between faculty and students?
- What is the faculty/student ratio?
- What research projects are faculty engaged in?
- What percentage of the faculty are tenured?

> **Tenure** *Tenure* means a faculty member has a permanent position at the graduate school. There is a great deal of competition for tenure, which is granted after several years of successful performance.

- What are the average or median GPA and GRE test scores of the most recent entering class?
- What are your chances for admission?
- What are the job placement and student advisory services like?
- What is the career outlook for graduates from this program?
- Are there many nontraditional students?
- Are there special services for nontraditional students?
- What kind of assistantships are available?
- What kind of fieldwork opportunities are available?
- What are the library, laboratory, and research facilities like?

How to Ask Questions

Here are some suggestions that will help when you are asked if you have any questions:

- Read the catalog carefully so you won't ask questions that have already been answered.
- Use the catalog as a jumping-off point; seek to clarify issues it raises.
- Write your questions down before the interview and refer to them during the interview.
- Never say you have no questions.
- Don't interrupt the interviewer in the middle of an answer.
- Ask follow-up questions for greater depth.

Types of Questions You May Be Asked

Here are some questions you may be asked during your interview:

- What are your reasons for wanting to pursue graduate study?
- Why are you applying to this program?
- What are your career goals?
- What contribution can you make to this field?
- Why does your specialty interest you?
- What is your greatest strength?
- What is your greatest weakness?

- What achievement are you proudest of to date?
- What is an example of a problem you have faced and solved?
- Does your college transcript accurately reflect your ability? If not, why not?
- Why did you change your college major?
- Do you have any related work experience?
- What is your opinion of the latest trends in your field?

How to Answer Questions

Here are some suggestions that will help you answer questions:

- Be courteous at all times.
- Don't answer with a straight "Yes" or "No."
- If you are asked questions on controversial issues (like politics, religion, abortion, and so on) or "stress" questions, remain calm and unflustered. Most interviewers simply want to assess your reasoning skills.
- Be prepared to explain an answer.
- Think before you speak. Don't answer impulsively.

General Interview Tips

Follow these tips to have a successful interview:

- Dress professionally and neatly.
- Bring a resume or transcript with you.

- Arrive promptly or early.
- Introduce any relative or friend who may be with you.
- Shake the interviewer's hand firmly.
- Smile and greet the interviewer pleasantly.
- Send a thank-you letter afterward. Refer to a point or two made at the interview, and name all the other people you met at the graduate school to distinguish yourself in the interviewer's mind.

AUDITIONS

Programs in music, dance, and theater usually require an audition to prove your talent and skills. Read catalogs carefully for requirements, such as whether it should be live or taped, whether it should be memorized, what constitutes appropriate repertoire and length, etc. Performance majors (such as dance) set higher standards than nonperformance majors (such as dance education), and regard the audition as the most crucial part of your application.

SUMMARY

In this lesson you learned questions to ask, questions you may be asked, and tips on how to handle interviews. You also learned the importance of auditions in arts programs.

LESSON 11

Paying for Graduate School

In this lesson you will learn about the graduate school financial aid process and the key factors to consider when applying for financial aid.

Applying for Financial Aid

As soon as you decide to apply to graduate school, you must explore sources of financial aid. The financial aid application process runs parallel to the graduate school admissions process. You will be applying for admissions and funding at the same time.

tip

Financial Application Musts Financial aid officers will tell you the key factors in obtaining financial aid are to:

- Apply as soon as possible
- Meet all application requirements and deadlines
- Explore and follow up on all applications

FOLLOWING A BASIC STRATEGY

Ideally, you will start exploring financial aid sources at least one and one-half years before starting school. During this research period you will obtain as much information as possible, assess your finances, and save additional monies for your education, if possible. Follow these steps:

1. Contact the financial aid office, graduate school admissions office, and individual department for each school and program you are applying to or are considering applying to.
2. Discuss the school's financial aid application requirements with the financial aid administrator and obtain several copies of all necessary applications, including the Free Application for Federal Student Aid (FAFSA) form.
3. Practice filling out the FAFSA in pencil. The FAFSA is the most commonly used financial aid application. It is also the most difficult to fill out. The FAFSA is used to apply for all federal aid and for a great deal of school and state aid. It may be the only form your school uses.
4. Ask the financial aid officer about alternate aid sources.
5. Ask the staff at the graduate school admissions office and individual department about financial assistance.
6. Explore outright awards (monies that do not have to be repaid) through your own research.

Figure 11.1 shows you different sources of financial aid.

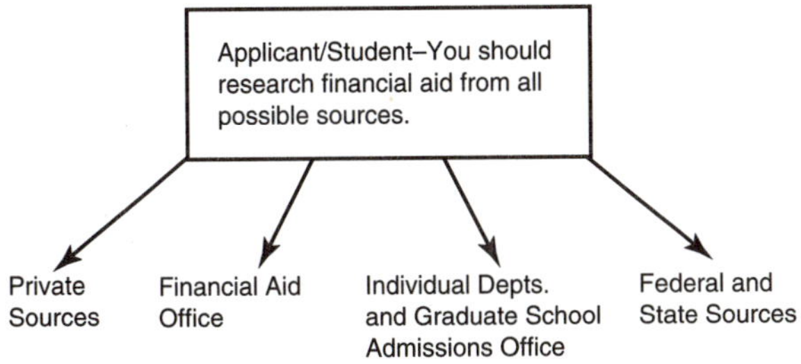

FIGURE 11.1 Sources of financial aid.

UNDERSTANDING FINANCIAL AID

Aid available to you from government, school, and private sources is normally classified as need- or non-need–based aid, with merit-based and targeted aid usually considered as categories of non-need–based aid. As a graduate student, you are considered independent, and it may be easier for you to prove financial need at the graduate school level than it was for undergraduate study.

The following list defines the common types of financial aid:

- *Assistantships:* Financial aid given for working on-campus, usually on a part-time basis. Assistantships are usually merit-based, although need may be taken into account. Aid may be received in the form of paychecks or tuition waivers or reductions. Teaching, research, and administrative assistantships are extremely sought-after forms of financial aid.
- *Loans:* Loans are monies that have to be repaid with interest. Educational loans exist from government, school, and private sources. Federal low-interest educational loans are usually considered the best loans for graduate students.

- *Grants, Fellowships, and Scholarships:* Outright awards (monies that do not have to be repaid) from government, school, or private sources.
- *Work-study:* Term applied to student work arrangements providing on- or off-campus employment. Federal Work-Study (FWS) is need-based.
- *Need-based Aid:* Aid awarded on the basis of financial need. Need is usually determined by the Federal Methodology (FM) formula, which is used to determine federal and, in many cases, state aid. Universities may use this or a different formula for determining need. The FM formula as diagrammed in Figure 11.2 is Cost of Attendance minus Expected Family Contribution (your student contribution) equals Financial Need.

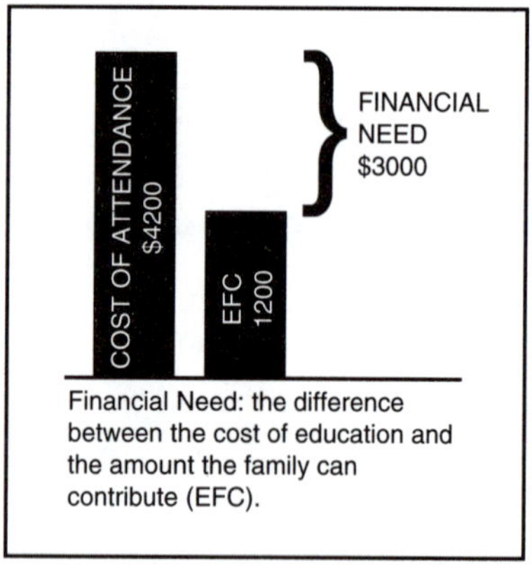

FIGURE 11.2 Federal Methodology formula.

- *Merit-based Aid:* Aid awarded on the basis of merit. High undergraduate GPAs and standardized test scores can be strong determinants in your eligibility for merit-based aid.

- *Targeted Aid:* Financial aid earmarked for certain groups—students pursuing specific areas of study; minorities and women; veterans, disabled, and foreign students; U.S. students studying abroad. Targeted aid can be need- or merit-based or a combination of the two.

Questions You Must Ask

Work closely with the financial aid officer to meet all requirements. The financial aid office will be your primary source of information about obtaining financial aid. The following is a checklist of questions you should get answers to as soon as possible.

- What is the deadline for financial aid applications?
- Does this deadline apply to all forms of aid or are there other deadlines?
- What forms do you require besides the Free Application for Federal Student Aid (FAFSA)?
- Do you provide all necessary applications? If not, where can I obtain them?
- Do you file the FAFSA electronically?
- What is the average cost of attendance for the program I am interested in?
- What is the average financial award package?
- What is the breakdown of the package between loans and outright awards (monies that do not have to be repaid)?
- Am I entitled to state financial aid? (If you are a nonresident student, be sure to ask this question.)

- How can I apply for state residency requirements?
- How do I apply for state aid?
- Where do I obtain state financial aid applications?
- What are the phone numbers of the state's Student Financial Aid Office and the State Guaranty Agency?

State Guaranty Agency The state agency responsible for administering educational loans. In some cases, it is the same agency as the Student Financial Aid Office.

MANAGING APPLICATION DEADLINES

It is critical that you meet the financial aid application deadlines from all sources you seek out. For many programs, your chances of getting funding depends on the availability of funding. Therefore, the earlier you apply, the better. It is your job to stay on top of and manage the financial aid application process by:

- Continually asking questions to ensure that you have the right information.
- Obtaining the correct applications, filling them in accurately and neatly, and submitting them on time with all required documentation.
- Promptly attending to all mail and queries from the school and all sources you are applying to.

tip

Write Down All Dates As early as possible, prepare a calendar of all dates you must meet and verify that these dates are correct. Remember, financial aid deadlines do not necessarily coincide with school admission deadlines; in many cases, they come earlier. Federal, state, and private financial aid application deadlines differ. Either use a yearly calendar you can write on or prepare your own monthly worksheets. Review each month's worksheet the month before to ensure you're getting in your applications as scheduled.

UNDERSTANDING FINANCIAL AID PACKAGES

You will be notified by schools if you are eligible or ineligible for financial aid. However, you will only receive an award letter after

- You are accepted for admission, and
- You have met all the financial aid application requirements.

It is extremely important that you read and understand the award letter before accepting an offer. Always call the financial aid office if you do not understand the conditions of the package.

tip

Awards Must Be Carefully Assessed When deciding among award packages, you should set up a comparison chart to evaluate the differences in packages. Be sure to consider all factors, including:

- The package with the lowest overall costs
- The packages with the least unmet need (monies you are eligible for but which the school is unable to fund)
- The different terms and conditions for all loans awarded
- The schools offering the best outright awards that do not have to be repaid
- The schools that in your opinion will provide the best education

SUMMARY

In this lesson you learned important strategies for financial aid applications, the main types of financial aid available, and methods for assessing financial aid packages.

LESSON 12

GETTING GRANTS, SCHOLARSHIPS, AND OTHER FUNDING

In this lesson you will learn how to research and apply for one of the most attractive types of financial assistance—outright awards—in order to finance your education.

GETTING OUTRIGHT AWARDS

It is up to you to seek out, research, and apply for most of the outright awards that are available for graduate study. Because competition for many awards is fierce and the application deadlines come early, you should begin your research as soon as possible.

Outright Awards Monies that do not have to be repaid. Such awards can take the form of grants, fellowships, and scholarships. Some outright awards have a service-related component.

The following list identifies potential sources of outright awards.

- Universities
- Federal and state government
- Your employer
- Foundations and corporations
- Unions and labor groups
- Professional, nonprofit, and educational associations
- Civic and religious groups
- Cultural and ethnic associations

tip

Advantages of Outright Gifts Outright awards come in all shapes and sizes—from small stipends to fellowships that cover your entire tuition. Since you should borrow as little money as possible to finance your graduate degree, it makes sense to apply for all outright awards that you are qualified for.

Doing Your Homework

Besides providing you with information on its own awards, each school should be an important information resource on other funding sources. Use the following checklist to query the financial aid office, graduate school admission office, and individual department.

- What awards do I automatically apply for by submitting my school financial aid application?
- Are there other awards available through my department or program?
- How do I apply for them?
- When are the application deadlines?
- Is there a dedicated Grants Officer on staff to assist me?
- What information resources—from directories to Internet sites—does the school provide?
- How can I obtain or access them?
- How does the school treat awards from outside sources in determining financial aid eligibility?

In addition, you should research directories and publications for information about outright awards. At the end of this lesson, you will find a detailed bibliography and resource list for exploring grants, fellowships, and scholarships.

Application Strategies

Each award will have its own requirements, and the amount of paperwork required will differ. Merit-based awards will probably not require you to demonstrate financial need. Remember to write down all deadline information on your monthly worksheet (see Lesson 11) to ensure that you get your application in on time. Use the following checklist to keep track of the requirements for each award.

1. Must I write an essay or personal statement?
   Yes___No___
2. If yes, how many? What topics are required?
3. Is an interview required? Yes___No___
4. Are personal letters of recommendation required?
   Yes___No___
5. If yes, how many? Must the recommendation writers be somehow affiliated with the award sponsor?
6. Is a resume or curriculum vitae required?
   Yes___No___
7. What transcripts are required? Academic?
   Yes___No___ Financial? Yes___No___
8. Are standardized test scores required? Yes___No___
9. If yes, which tests?
10. Must I submit my last year's tax return? Yes___No___
11. Must I submit my parents' last year's tax return?
    Yes___No___
12. Are specific application forms required? Yes___No___
13. Is an application fee required? Yes___No___
14. Must I prepare an in-depth proposal? Yes___No___
15. Must I be nominated from specific sources?
    Yes___No___

FIGURE 12.1 Outright award requirements checklist.

tip **Follow Directions Carefully** You should be extremely careful when preparing your application. Be sure to answer every question directly and honestly. If possible, have someone else proofread your work. Get all of the required documentation together ahead of time to beat the deadlines.

Application Writing Guidelines

Whether your application calls for a short or lengthy essay, you want to ensure your work meets the highest possible standards. Use the following questions as your writing guide.

- Is my work carefully structured? Do all points lead to a logical conclusion?
- Is the writing objective and well thought out? Have I included everything I need to?
- Do I back up all points with concrete examples to state my case?
- Is my prose style easy to read?
- Have I adhered to the specified page limit or word count?

Preparing Lengthy Proposals

At some point in your graduate school career, you may have to prepare a substantive proposal to obtain funding and to secure major grants or fellowships. Following is one suggested proposal format. When preparing your proposal, keep the sponsor's requirements in mind and seek the counsel of your faculty adviser.

Table 12.1 Essential Proposal Components

Component Name	Content of Component
1. Summary/Abstract	Provides a concise summary of the proposal including amount of funding requested.
2. Introduction	Provides essential background information including applicant's history, qualifications, activities, and accomplishments. States important research and findings in your area and what your project will contribute to this body of knowledge.
3. Problem-Statement	Discusses and documents the needs or problems to be solved by the funding.
4. Objectives	Provides concrete statements on how the problem or need will be addressed, giving timelines and measurable criteria.
5. Methods	States how you will accomplish your objectives, including activities to be done, reasons for your approach, and any special requirements you may need.
6. Evaluation	States how your objectives will be assessed, how data will be collected, and how results will be used.
7. Budget	Presents a clear breakdown and itemization of the costs of the project.

Do Your Research

Your library is the best avenue of research since many grants and scholarship directories are annual publications and extremely expensive. Many financial aid offices will keep directories for reference. Some resources include:

- *Annual Register of Grant Support.* R.R. Bowker: New York, NY.
- *Catalog of Federal Domestic Assistance.* U.S. Government Printing Office: Washington, D.C.
- *Directory of Financial Aids for Minorities.* Reference Service Press: Santa Barbara, CA.
- *Directory of Financial Aids for Women.* Reference Service Press: Santa Barbara, CA.
- *Directory of Research Grants.* Oryx Press: Scottsdale, AZ.
- *Financial Aid for the Disabled and Their Families.* Reference Service Press: Santa Barbara, CA.
- *Financial Aid for Veterans, Military Personnel, and Their Families.* Reference Service Press: Santa Barbara, CA.
- *Foundation Directory.* The Foundation Center: New York, NY.
- *Foundation Grants to Individuals.* The Foundation Center: New York, NY.
- *Free Money for Graduate School.* Henry Holt: New York, NY.
- *The Grants Register.* St. Martins: New York, NY.
- *Lesko's Info-Power.* Gale Research: Detroit, MI.
- *Worldwide Graduate Scholarship Directory.* Career Press: Franklin Lakes, NJ.

Getting Employer Assistance

If you are employed, find out whether your employer sponsors tuition assistance programs. Ask a Human Resources representative about your employer's policies for graduate study and how they apply to you in your current position. Employee tuition benefits are often unused because people are unaware of their availability.

If you know any colleagues at work who are currently in school or have obtained a graduate degree, speak to them. It will help you weigh the advantages and disadvantages of holding down a full-time job while going to graduate school.

You may want to ask your employer the following questions:

- Will getting a graduate degree help me in my current position?
- Can an advanced degree lead to job promotions within my department or elsewhere within the company?
- Are there any programs or courses of study that my employer will not contribute to?
- As a part-time student, will my employer be flexible if I need to leave work early?
- Can I take time off from work to attend intensive summer programs or seminars?

Summary

In this lesson you learned about public and private sources of outright awards, outright award application strategies, and employer assistance for graduate study.

LESSON 13

Working to Pay for Your Education

In this lesson you will learn about different work-study opportunities available to graduate students.

Getting Service-Related Awards

Merit- and need-based service-related awards offer students excellent funding opportunities. The following list introduces you to the service-related awards you should seek out.

- *Administrative Assistantship.* Work-study arrangement where you provide supporting services to specific departments.
- *Assistantship.* Financial aid provided for performing work, usually on a part-time basis. Assistantships are usually awarded according to merit.
- *Cooperative Education.* Work-study arrangement where you receive academic credit for work outside of school. You will work as a salaried employee for a participating company.

- *Federal Work-Study (FWS).* Federal subsidy program that provides jobs for students demonstrating financial need. FWS encourages community service work and work related to your course of study.
- *Internship.* Work-study arrangement allowing you to gain practical experience through off-campus work with participating companies. In some cases, you can receive payment from the participating organizations.
- *Research Assistantship.* Work helping professors do research, carry out experiments, and analyze data. These positions are common in scientific fields.
- *Residence Assistantship.* Work where you help out in undergraduate dormitories and receive free room and board for your service.
- *Service-Related Grant/Fellowship.* Outright award that has a service component, e.g., carrying on specific research.
- *Teaching Assistantship.* Work where you help professors read and grade papers, run seminars, and tutor small groups.

tip

Seek Out Assistantships Many assistantships are extremely prized by students. They may offer you the chance to:

- Work in your field of study
- Gain valuable teaching or work experience
- Make important contacts in your area

When applying for financial aid, explore obtaining assistantships through the financial aid office, graduate admission office, and individual departments. Know what the requirements and deadlines are and be sure to meet them. Since many assistantships are awarded by the department, you should cultivate faculty contacts by interviewing faculty when you are deciding on a graduate school.

TABLE 13.1 AVERAGE VALUE OF ASSISTANTSHIPS

	FULL-TIME	PART-TIME
Master's students	$6,342	$5,921
Doctoral students	$9,203	$7,722

Source: Student Financing of Graduate and First-Professional Education, U.S. Department of Education, 1993

tip

Explore Cooperative Education and Internships Both can provide you with excellent work experience in your field of study. To find out more about cooperative education programs, contact the National Center for Cooperative Education, Northeastern University, 360 Huntington Avenue, Boston, MA. Tel: 617-437-3778.

To find out more about internship programs, contact the financial aid office or individual department.

UNDERSTANDING FEDERAL WORK-STUDY

This is one of several federal financial aid programs you apply for when you fill out the FAFSA application for federal aid. It is only available to students who demonstrate financial need and only at participating institutions. While wages for FWS jobs are low, FWS may offer you work relevant to your field of study. If you are given a work-study award, always:

- Consult with the financial aid office on how to conduct your job search
- Work with the school to find jobs in your area of study
- Clear your job with the school financial aid office before accepting the position.

> *tip*
>
> **Get Part-time Work** If you are unable to secure any of the above aid and need additional money to make ends meet, check with your student employment office and financial aid office about on- and off-campus jobs. The employment office often serves as a clearinghouse for local work opportunities.

SUMMARY

In this lesson you learned about getting assistantships, researching cooperative education and internships, and applying for Federal Work-Study.

LESSON 14

Borrowing Money

In this lesson you will learn about public and private loan sources and the pros and cons of borrowing money to finance your degree.

Borrowing Money for Graduate School

You will probably have to borrow some money to finance your graduate education. Financial aid advisers suggest that you be realistic and take on as little debt as possible. For as soon as you get out of school, in most cases, you must start making repayments.

> *tip* **Always Research Government Loans** Federal aid through the form of low-interest loans has become the graduate student's main source of financial aid. Your financial aid award package will tell you what loans you are entitled to. Federal loans offer the best interest rates around and even payment deferment and cancellation provisions under certain conditions. State loans are also attractive loan sources and may offer terms similar to federal loans.

ATTRACTIVE GOVERNMENT LOAN FEATURES

As a graduate student, you are considered independent for financial aid purposes and you will probably meet federal guidelines for financial aid eligibility. However, even if you think you are ineligible (e.g., you are employed full-time and will be going to school on a part-time basis) you should still explore government loans because:

1. Federal Unsubsidized Stafford Loans (see next page) are non-need–based and will probably offer you better interest rates than private loans, and
2. For state educational loans, if your state's need formula is different than the federal one, need may be easier to prove.

OBTAINING LOAN INFORMATION

The financial aid office must offer you counseling and will provide a great deal of loan information if you are borrowing money. Figure 14.1 shows recommended subjects you should discuss at your entrance interview (when you begin school) and exit interview (before you leave school). Items in the core section should be addressed at both interviews.

Some of these items may not be covered in your interview, so it is up to you to bring them up. Use Figure 14.1 as a checklist to get all the information you require.

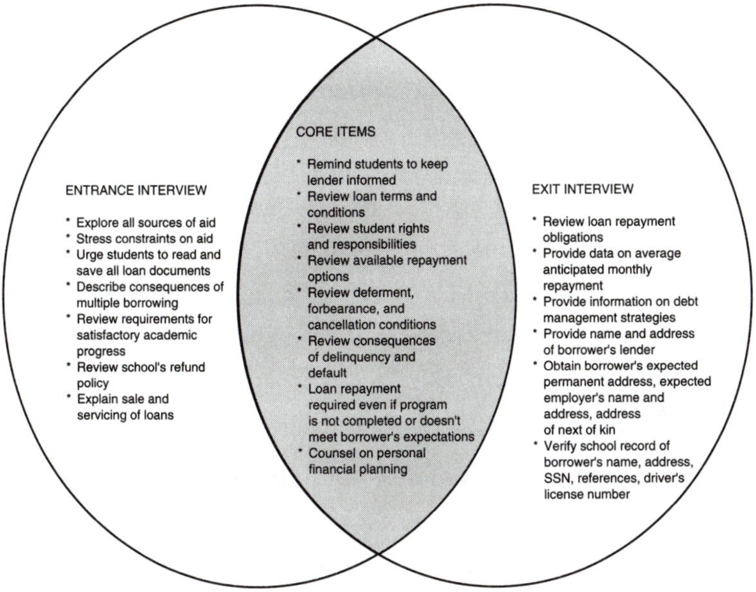

FIGURE 14.1 Checklist of interview information.

Most Common Federal Educational Loans

There are three major types of federal loans available for graduate study: (1) Perkins Loans, (2) Subsidized Stafford Loans, and (3) Unsubsidized Stafford Loans. Perkins loans are awarded to students demonstrating exceptional financial need, subsidized Stafford Loans are awarded on the basis of financial need, and unsubsidized Stafford Loans are non-need–based.

BEST SOURCE OF GOVERNMENT HELP

For immediate answers to questions about federal student aid, call the Federal Student Aid Information Center between 9 a.m. and 8 p.m. Monday through Friday at 1-800-4-FED-AID (1-800-433-3243) or 1-800-730-913 for the hearing impaired. The center will:

- Send you federal student aid publications, including the *Student Guide to Financial Aid,* which clearly explains all federal loan and aid programs
- Explain federal student aid eligibility requirements
- Explain the process of determining financial need and awarding aid
- Assist you in completing the federal student financial aid application
- Tell you whether a school participates in federal student aid programs

PROMISSORY NOTES

As a borrower, you should never borrow more than you need. This applies to all types of loans, both government and private (see following page). As a borrower, you will sign a binding legal agreement—a *promissory note*—that lists the conditions under which you're borrowing and the terms of repayment.

Promissory Note—Federal Perkins Loan Program

I, ______(your name)______, promise to pay to (your school) ______(hereinafter called the Institution), located at ______ (school's location)______, the sum of the amounts that are advanced to me and endorsed in the Schedule of Advances set forth below. I promise to pay all reasonable collection costs, including attorney's fees and other charges, necessary for the collection of any amount not paid when due.

I further understand and agree that:

I. General

(1)Applicable Law. All sums advanced under this note are drawn from a fund created under Part E of Title IV of the Higher Education Act of 1965, as amended...

Figure 14.2 Excerpt from a promissory note—Federal Perkins Loan Program.

Remember that while you can borrow a fair amount of money under the Stafford Loan programs for graduate and professional school, you should always explore the outright awards discussed in Lesson 12. Table 14.1 shows you the loan limits for Stafford Loans.

Table 14.1 Loan Limits for Subsidized and Unsubsidized Stafford Loans

Loan Type	Annual Limit	Cumulative Limit
Stafford Loans Subsidized	$8,500	$65,500—includes amounts borrowed for undergraduate study
Stafford Loans Unsubsidized	$10,000	$138,000—includes amounts borrowed for undergraduate study

SECURING OTHER LOANS

If you do not qualify for government loans or need additional money to cover your graduate school expenses, seek out the best loan packages through schools and educational loan programs as well as commercial lenders such as banks, savings and loans, credit unions, and finance companies.

tip

Check on School and Private Programs Find out from the financial aid office whether your school offers no-interest monthly payment plans or a low-interest loan payment program. The financial aid office can also supply you with information on several national educational loan programs that offer a wide variety of loan programs.

!

Always Compare Commercial Lenders Always shop around for deals. Your aim is to find the loan with the lowest interest rates and borrowing charges (including origination and insurance fees). As a consumer, compare loan rates carefully. Don't hesitate to ask your bank to beat a better offer.

SUMMARY

In this lesson you learned about the different types of government loans available for graduate school, commercial and private loan sources, and how to get loan information through your school's financial aid office.

LESSON 15

PREPARING FOR THE GRE GENERAL TEST

In this lesson you will learn about the GRE General Test and will be given an overview of the exam, general test-taking advice, and information on the two GRE formats—the traditional pencil-and-paper version and the new computer adaptive test (CAT).

GETTING STARTED

Get your complete GRE information kit from Educational Testing Service (ETS) as soon as you start exploring graduate school. The kit will give you detailed information on:

- Test registration and administrative services including advice for disabled students, other student groups, and special test-taking arrangements
- Fees for tests and services
- Score reporting and score cancellation policies
- Test dates
- Test content with sample questions and suggested test-taking strategies

Information and registration packets may also be available in your college and graduate school financial aid and admissions offices. Call or write ETS at:

Graduate Record Examinations
Educational Testing Service
P.O. Box 6000
Princeton, NJ 08541-6000

609-771-7670 (Princeton, NJ),
Monday-Friday, 8:30am–9:00pm, EST

510-873-8100 (Oakland, CA),
Monday-Friday, 8:15am–4:30pm, PST

> *tip* **Phone for Quick Information** Since you must allow four to six weeks for a mail response, use the phone. Callers with touch-tone phones can use the recorded phone service available 24 hours a day.

Understanding GRE General Test Format

Today, the GRE General Test is offered in two formats: (1) traditional paper-and-pencil version, and (2) computer adaptive test (CAT). Both test your skill in answering multiple choice questions in verbal, quantitative, and analytical areas.

While the content of the two versions of the GRE General Test is nearly the same, there are certain format, scoring, and administration differences. Tables 15.1 and 15.2 compare the formats and time limits for the pencil-and-paper GRE versus the computer version.

TABLE 15.1 TYPICAL PENCIL-AND-PAPER GRE*

SECTION	NO. OF QUESTIONS	TIME LIMIT
Verbal	38	30 minutes
Quantitative	30	30 minutes
Analytical	25	30 minutes
Verbal	38	30 minutes
Quantitative	30	30 minutes
Analytical	25	30 minutes
Research**	—	30 minutes

**Ordering of sections including the research section varies from administration to administration.*

***Research section is not scored.*

TABLE 15.2 TYPICAL GRE COMPUTER-ADAPTIVE TEST (CAT)*

SECTION	NUMBER OF QUESTIONS	MINIMUM NUMBER OF ANSWERS REQUIRED FOR A SCORE	TIME LIMIT
Pretest			n/a
Verbal	30	24	30 minutes
Quantitative	28	23	45 minutes
Analytical	35	28	60 minutes
Research			n/a

**Ordering of sections including Pretest will vary from administration to administration. If a research section is included, it will always be the last section of the test.*

DECIDING WHICH VERSION IS BEST FOR YOU

The big advantage of the computer test is its convenience:

- You can take it nearly anytime you want at more than 225 testing centers
- You get your scores immediately and schools will receive them in about two to three weeks after you take the test

However, the computer test has many drawbacks, including:

- Expense—it will cost you more to take it
- Narrower test-taking strategies—many traditional test-taking strategies will not apply (this and following lessons will give you test-taking strategies)
- Possibility of eye fatigue—reading a computer terminal for three hours steadily can wear you out
- Limited retaking opportunities—you may take the CAT only once within a six-month period

While the computer test will eventually replace the other version, the pencil-and-paper version is still easier for most people. The advantages of the paper-and-pencil test are:

- It is less expensive to take
- It can be retaken at any of the announced administration dates

tip

Obtain Test Fee Waivers Basic fees for the paper-and-pencil and CAT versions of the GRE are $64 and $96, respectively. Currently the GRE

Board provides a fee waiver service for both versions of the test. Check with your undergraduate or graduate school financial aid office to see if you are eligible. Since only a limited number of waivers are available, do this as soon as possible.

SCORING INFORMATION

The GRE is scored on a scale of 200 (minimum) to 800 (maximum). You will receive three separate scores for each subsection: Verbal, Quantitative (Math), and Analytical. There is no penalty for guessing; nothing is deducted from your score if you answer a question incorrectly.

For the pencil-and-paper GRE, your score is based on the number of items answered correctly. For the computer test, your score is based on your performance—more credit is given for correctly answering difficult questions than easy ones. ETS states that CAT scores are comparable to pencil-and-paper scores.

Scoring or Guessing Penalty Since you are not penalized for incorrectly answered questions on the GRE, you should guess when necessary.

Table 15.3 shows the average scores obtained by recent GRE test-takers.

TABLE 15.3 RECENT AVERAGE GRE GENERAL TEST SCORES*

YEAR	NO. OF TEST-TAKERS	VERBAL	QUANTITATIVE	ANALYTICAL
1988	303,703	483	557	528
1989	326,096	484	560	530
1990	344,572	486	562	534
1991	379,882	485	562	536
1992	411,528	483	561	537

**Source: Digest of Educational Statistics, 1994.*

GENERAL TEST-TAKING SKILL AND STRATEGIES

The best test-taking strategy for either version of the GRE is to practice taking a simulated GRE as often as possible.

You should thoroughly understand the strategies and directions for each question type before taking the test. (The directions used for sample GRE questions in this book are substantially the same as those on the actual GRE.)

In addition, the confidence that you will achieve with repeated practice will help you on the actual test. The GRE registration booklet will give you information on ordering official ETS exam study materials. In addition, Arco offers a full line of GRE test preparation guides (listed in the Introduction). You should start studying at least three months before your test date.

> *tip*
>
> **Take Test Preparation Courses** If you have been out of school for several years or need to review certain test areas, you should seriously consider enrolling in an exam preparation course. Getting higher test scores will help you gain admittance to competitive programs and also make you a stronger contender for merit-based aid. Check with your school for recommended test prep courses in your area.

The following list offers test-taking strategies for the paper-and-pencil GRE.

- Do not waste time reading directions when you take the actual test—you should already know them.
- Work quickly—practice will give you this ability. Since all questions are of equal value, you should not become obsessed with any one question.
- Be sure you bring a watch to the test to keep track of time.
- Eliminate inappropriate answer choices before answering a question. The multiple-choice test format allows you to do this.
- If in doubt, guess—there is no guessing penalty.
- Fill in the answer sheet carefully—stray marks could be interpreted as your answer.
- Within test sections, skip questions you don't know or which will take more time. Come back to them to guess or work them out when you've answered all other questions.

- In verbal sections, save reading comprehension for last.
- In quantitative sections, do quantitative comparisons first, leave graph questions for last.
- In analytical sections, do logical reasoning questions first.
- For those questions that only have four answer choices (A through D), be certain you don't enter an E on your answer sheet.

The following list gives you strategies for taking the test on computer.

- Work through the CAT tutorials carefully—take as much time as you think necessary to become comfortable with the format.
- Become comfortable with scrolling before you take the test. Since some question types will be too large to appear completely on the screen, you will have to scroll through the text to read them.
- Do your best to answer each question in the order it is presented. You cannot skip questions and return to them later. Choose the best answer, quickly recheck your work, and move on.
- Be certain you have answered the minimum number of questions required to get a score.
- If time is running out, guess judiciously but not randomly. You are better leaving the last few questions unanswered than randomly guessing.
- Keep track of time by checking the computer screen.

> **Remember 1999** ETS now says that in 1999 the CAT will replace the paper-and-pencil test. This may or may not be the case. However, you will not have an option to choose between the two versions once the takeover occurs. So keep on top of test notices and start your exam preparation as early as possible.

SUMMARY

In this lesson you learned about the two different GRE general test formats, how to get information from ETS, and skills and strategies needed for taking the examination.

LESSON 16

Preparing for the Verbal Sections—Part 1

In this lesson you will learn about the three types of verbal ability questions on the Graduate Record Examination, and be provided with question-answering strategies to achieve higher test scores.

What the Verbal Ability Questions Test

The Education Testing Service (ETS) states that the verbal questions test your ability to reason with words in order to solve problems. You must be able to understand word or word group relationships within sentences, paragraphs, and written passages.

The four types of verbal questions are: analogies, antonyms, sentence completions, and reading comprehension.

There are two verbal sections on a paper-and-pencil GRE. Each section has 38 questions and is 30 minutes long. Table 16.1 shows the order of question types within a verbal section and the suggested order for answering them.

TABLE 16.1 VERBAL ABILITY SECTION ARRANGEMENT BY QUESTION TYPE

QUESTION TYPE	QUESTION NUMBERS	WHEN TO ANSWER THEM
Sentence Completions	1–7	Answer them first
Analogies	8–16	Answer them second
Reading Comprehension	17–27	Answer them last (fourth)
Antonyms	28–38	Answer them third

SKILLS YOU CAN USE

While specific test-taking strategies are listed in upcoming sections, certain general skills will better prepare you for answering verbal ability questions:

- *Strengthen your vocabulary*. Having a strong vocabulary will help you do better on all the verbal questions, especially antonyms. Use specialized vocabulary lists, study vocabulary building techniques, and increase your everyday reading to bolster your word power. Arco's GRE test preparation books (listed in the Introduction to this book) provide excellent study materials. You should also consider using the *10 Minute Guide to Building Your Vocabulary* (Alpha, 1997) and *Webster's New World Power Vocabulary* (Macmillan, 1994) to build your knowledge of English word components.
- *Read more specialized materials*. In addition to newspapers, read more specialized magazines and nonfiction works. GRE reading passages are informative but dull. Steep yourself in some new publications and look up words and terms you do not know.

Understanding Sentence Completion Questions

Sentence completion questions measure your ability to understand sentence meaning, syntax, and grammar. You have to analyze the relationships among parts of an incomplete sentence and choose the answer that best completes the sentence logically and stylistically. Study the sentence completion in Figure 16.1.

> *Directions:* The following sentence contains one or two blank spaces, indicating that something has been omitted. Following it are five words or sets of words. Choose the word or set of words which, when inserted in the sentence, best fits the meaning of the sentence.
>
> As a dancer, she sought__________in her art, practicing her routines over and over again until they seemed flawless.
>
> (A) dislocation
> (B) perfection
> (C) detection
> (D) defeat
> (E) allocation
>
> The best answer is **(B)**. The logic of the sentence requires that the missing word show what is achieved by the dancer's constant practice. If your work is flawless, in effect, it is perfect.

Figure 16.1 Sample sentence completion.

Now study the following strategies for solving sentence completions.

- Read the sentence quickly and carefully, looking for shades of meaning. Try to anticipate the answers that will work.
- Use your own word choices to fill in the blanks. Then find the answer choice that matches yours.
- Notice sentence grammar and structure. Make sure the answer choice makes sense in terms of logic and meaning.
- For sentences with two blanks, make sure that both choices work.
- When guessing, eliminate all obviously incorrect answers before making your choice.

Understanding Analogy Questions

Analogy questions test your ability to understand the relationship between a pair of words and choose a word pair that expresses a similar relationship. Study the analogy in Figure 16.2.

Directions: The following question shows a related pair of words or phrases followed by five lettered pairs of words or phrases. Choose the lettered pair that best expresses a relationship similar to that expressed by the original pair.

SONNET:POEM::

(A) credit:movie
(B) envelope:letter
(C) ballad:song
(D) melody:rhythm
(E) ode:dance

The best answer is **(C)**. In this common type of analogy, a sonnet is a type of poem and a ballad is a type of song.

Figure 16.2 Sample analogy.

The following are strategies for solving analogies.

- Read the question quickly and try to establish a definite relationship between the original word pair. Look at your answer choices to see if any of them expresses that same relationship.
- Refine your analogy relationship by looking at secondary word meanings and indirect word relationships.
- Never make a selection without reading all answer choices.

tip **Determine Analogy Relationships** There are several types of analogy relationships that ETS frequently uses in analogy questions. Some relationship categories are: size, degree, kind, part, cause and effect, and spatial dimension. Use the Arco books listed in the Introduction as a guide to understanding analogy categories. The more practice you have, the easier analogy questions will become.

UNDERSTANDING ANTONYM QUESTIONS

Antonym questions test your vocabulary skills and your ability to deduce words and ideas that are opposite in meaning to the original concept. Study the antonyms in Figure 16.3.

Directions: The following question consists of a word printed in capital letters followed by five lettered words or phrases. Choose the word or phrase that is most nearly opposite in meaning to the capitalized word.

OPAQUE

(A) easily accomplished
(B) overly polite
(C) gently sloping
(D) pleasantly sweet
(E) readily understood

The answer is **(E)**. Opaque has several meanings. If you know that one meaning of the word is *unclear* or *hard to understand*, then (E) is your obvious answer.

FIGURE 16.3 Sample antonym.

Now look over the following strategies for solving antonyms.

- Try to define the meaning of the capitalized word quickly.
- When unsure of the meaning, try using vocabulary skills to derive word meaning. If you know the meaning of any word component—prefix, root, or suffix—you may be able to arrive at the word's meaning.
- If you have a vague idea of the word's meaning, eliminate obvious incorrect answers before guessing.

tip

Easiest Questions Appear First All three of the above question types are arranged within sections according to degree of difficulty. The easiest questions come first and you should breeze through them.

Summary

In this lesson you learned about verbal ability test sections and were provided with skills and strategies for answering three question types—sentence completions, analogies, and antonyms.

LESSON 17

Preparing for the Verbal Sections—Part 2

In this lesson you will learn strategies and guidelines for doing well on reading comprehension questions.

Testing Critical Reading Skills

Preparing for reading comprehension questions may actually benefit your graduate school work. As a graduate student, your reading and research may be in scholarly and arcane subjects. You will have to get to the heart of some extremely boring material. Think of these GRE questions as a dry run. The skills you need here will be invaluable in your actual studies.

Many GRE reading comprehension passages are drawn from different areas in the social, natural, and biological sciences, and the humanities, including:

- Science and technology
- Medicine
- Psychology
- Philosophy

- Sociology
- Economics
- Literary criticism
- History

UNDERSTANDING READING COMPREHENSION QUESTIONS

Reading comprehension tests your ability to understand and analyze a written passage, to make assumptions from statements made in the passage, and to draw conclusions from the implications of these statements. Study the sample question in Figure 17.1. (This reading passage is shorter than those you will encounter on the actual test.)

Directions: The passage below is followed by questions based on the content of the passage. Answer the questions on the basis of what is stated or meant by the passage.

Initial lifting to trigger a cumuliform cloud may be the same as that for lifting stable air. In addition, convection may be set off by surface heating. Air may be unstable or slightly stable before condensation occurs; but for convective cumuliform clouds to develop, it must be unstable after saturation. Cooling in the updraft is now at the slower moist adiabatic rate because of the release of latent heat of condensation. Temperature in the saturated updraft is warmer than ambient temperature, and convection is spontaneous. Updrafts accelerate until the temperature within the cloud cools below the ambient temperature. This condition occurs where the unstable layer is capped by a stable layer often marked by a temperature inversion. Vertical heights range from the shallow fair weather cumulus to the giant thunderstorm cumulonimbus—the ultimate in atmospheric instability capped by the tropopause.

What atmospheric condition is always necessary for convective cumuliform clouds to form?

(A) high ambient temperatures and stable air
(B) temperature inversion
(C) low ambient temperature and high adiabatic rate
(D) unstable air
(E) surface heating

The only answer to this question is **(D)**, which is clearly stated in sentence three. Choices (A) through (C) do not make sense in terms of the passage. (E) may be a factor some of the time.

Figure 17.1 Sample reading comprehension question using abbreviated passage.

Now look over the following strategies to increase your skill at reading comprehension questions.

- Do not be intimidated by a passage. All the information you will need to answer a question will be in the passage. You are not expected to be familiar with the material presented.
- Preview the entire passage by zooming in on the first sentence of each paragraph. First sentences are often topic sentences. This will give you an overview of the selection.

- Read each passage carefully—especially the first third—and always keep asking yourself:
  - "What is the main idea?"
  - "What conclusions are drawn?"
  - "How is the main idea supported?"
- Be certain you understand a question before answering it.
- Read each answer choice carefully before answering.
- Write in the test booklet, if necessary, to underline or bracket important points in the passage. While this may be against verbal test center directions, do not be afraid to do this.

tip

Do Reading Comprehension Questions Last
You will have two reading comprehension passages in each verbal section. The passages will vary in length—one will be about 60 lines, the other about 20 lines. The passages can be quite complex and you will need time to concentrate. As stated in Lesson 16, do reading comprehension questions last. There is no order of difficulty to question arrangements. Do the passage you feel most comfortable with first.

LEARNING CATEGORIES OF QUESTIONS

Knowing the question categories will help focus your energies on the actual test. The Educational Testing Service (ETS) lists six separate types of reading comprehension questions:

- *Main Idea or Primary Purpose.* You are asked about the central idea or theme of the passage.
- *Information Explicitly Stated.* You are asked about details mentioned by the author that support or develop the main theme of the selection.
- *Information Implied or Suggested.* You are asked about ideas that are strongly implied or suggested by the selection.
- *Further Application.* You are asked to apply the author's ideas to other situations, situations not stated or implied in the passage.
- *Logical Structure/Persuasive Techniques.* You are asked about the organization and development of a selection.
- *Tone and Attitude.* You are asked to identify the author's specific tone or attitude revealed through language.

SUMMARY

In this lesson you learned basic strategies for answering reading comprehension questions and were provided with categories of questions tested by ETS.

LESSON 18

Preparing for the Quantitative Sections

In this lesson you will learn about the quantitative portions of the GRE, and learn helpful test-taking tips and study advice to improve your basic math skills.

What Quantitative Ability Questions Test

ETS states that the quantitative ability questions measure your understanding of basic math skills and concepts, your ability to reason quantitatively, and your ability to solve math problems.

The content covers four broad areas:

- Arithmetic
- Algebra
- Geometry
- Data analysis

You will find two quantitative sections on the paper-and-pencil test, each containing 30 questions. Each section has two distinct question types, as shown in Table 18.1:

TABLE 18.1 QUANTITATIVE SECTION ARRANGEMENT BY QUESTION TYPE

QUESTION TYPE	QUESTION NUMBER	WHEN TO ANSWER THEM
Quantitative Comparison	1–15	Do first
Problem Solving	16–30	Do second

In addition, you will find graph and table questions within the problem-solving subsection. These problems should be answered last.

REVIEW YOUR MATH

While ETS states that the math required for the test does not go beyond that covered in high school, a certain amount of review will be necessary. How much will be determined by you. To get started:

- Review the GRE test booklet. It lists all concepts covered and sample test questions, including a full-length sample GRE.
- Review the math sections in the GRE books listed in the Introduction to this book. You will find diagnostic material to assess your strengths and weaknesses, review in all math areas, and drills to reinforce learning.
- If you need more of a refresher course or have more time to prepare, get additional study materials. One

highly recommended text is *GRE-GMAT Math Review* by David Frieder (Arco). This topic-by-topic review is geared toward test-takers and provides excellent instructional material.

The following list provides an overview of the subjects covered in the GRE math sections.

- *Arithmetic*: Real number operations of addition, subtraction, multiplication, division, and powers; fractions; decimals and percents; averages and proportions; rations; radicals; estimating; absolute value; and properties of numbers.
- *Algebra*: Relations and functions; expressions; exponents; factoring; equations with one and two variables; and quadratic equations.
- *Geometry*: Properties of figures including triangles, rectangles, and circles; area, perimeter, and volume; solids; measuring angles; and simple coordinate geometry.
- *Data Analysis*: Statistical concepts of mean, mode, median, range, and probability; and understanding and interpretation of graphic and tabular data.

Understanding Quantitative Comparison Questions

Quantitative comparison questions measure your ability to quickly assess the differences between two quantities and to judge whether the information provided in the problem is sufficient to solve the problem. Some quantitative comparison problems may not require you to solve the problem. Others may require more work. However, the key elements in successfully tackling these problems are to:

- Know the directions by heart.
- Understand what the directions mean.
- Be familiar with the format.

Study the sample quantitative comparison in Figure 18.1.

Directions: In each of the following questions, there are two quantities—one in Column A and one in Column B. Compare the two quantities and choose:

(A) if the quantity in Column A is the greater;

(B) if the quantity in Column B is the greater;

(C) if the two quantities are equal;

(D) if the relationship cannot be determined from the given information.

Note: Never mark (E), since there are only four answer choices.

Common Information: In any question, information applying to both columns is centered above the columns. The common information applies to both columns. Any symbol that appears in both columns represents the same idea or quantity in both columns.

Column A		Column B
	x is 3 more than y	
x		y

For the above question, the answer is **(A)**. Here your knowledge of the centered information is tested. If x is 3 more than y, then x must be larger than y. Therefore Column A must be larger than Column B.

FIGURE 18.1 Sample quantitative comparison.

Now review the following strategies.

- Do only as much work as necessary to solve the problem. When comparing quantities, you do not have to find exact sizes.
- Simplify complex numbers or expressions before making comparisons.
- For simple operations, work out the problems.
- With a question that contains unknowns, try substituting numbers.
- Redraw diagrams if they seem confusing. Geometric figures may not be drawn to scale.
- Consider all possibilities and all kinds of numbers before answering—numbers can be negative as well as positive.

UNDERSTANDING PROBLEM SOLVING QUESTIONS

Problem solving questions are standard multiple-choice math questions that you should be familiar with from previous tests like the SAT. The amount of computation called for by any problem depends on its complexity. Some problems require simple manipulation; some require you to thoroughly read and understand the problems before solving them. Study the sample problem-solving question in Figure 18.2.

Directions: For each of the following questions, choose the best answer choice. There are five answer choices per question.

Day	Mon	Tues	Wed	Thur	Fri
Sales	$40	$100	$80	$30	$50

What is the average (arithmetic mean) daily sales for the week shown above?

(A) $20
(B) $40
(C) $60
(D) $70
(E) $80

The answer is **(C)**. The most direct method for finding the average is to do the calculation required:

$40 + 100 + 80 + 30 + 50/5 = 300/5 = 60$

Figure 18.2 Sample problem-solving question.

Now study the following strategies.

- Read the question and answer choices carefully. Make sure you answer the question asked and that the units in your answer correspond to the units in the question.
- Always eliminate obvious incorrect answers before answering or guessing.
- Do not let problems with strange (nonmathematical) symbols intimidate you. The meaning of the symbol is always given in the question.

- If figures are noted as drawn to scale, use the figure to estimate your answer.
- The more difficult the question, the more difficult the solution. For such questions, eliminate answers determined by simple one-step operations.

tip

Easiest Questions Come First All quantitative comparison and problem-solving questions (except for graph and table problems) are arranged by order of difficulty.

Summary

In this lesson you learned how to review for the GRE math sections and how to tackle the two GRE math question types—quantitative comparisons and problem solving.

LESSON 19

Preparing for the Analytical Sections—Part 1

In this lesson you will learn about two types of analytical ability questions on the GRE and will acquire test-taking strategies for doing well on this section of your test.

What Analytical Ability Questions Test

The analytical ability questions have been designed to measure your ability to think logically in formal and informal ways. Unlike the other two GRE sections, there is no set ordering of analytical ability question types. Each analytical section will have 25 questions and can contain any of the following three question types:

- Logical reasoning
- Analytical reasoning (sometimes referred to by test prep coaches as "logical games")
- Analysis of explanations

Test coaches generally suggest doing logical reasoning questions first. Logical reasoning and analytical reasoning questions have the same directions. However, it is very easy to differentiate between the test questions on the actual test. The following list gives you an overview of the different questions.

- *Logical reasoning.* Logical reasoning questions ask you to analyze an argument, statement, graph, or table. Questions may be individual or in pairs.
- *Analytical reasoning.* Analytical reasoning questions are clustered in groups of three or more questions. The groups are based on a fictional situation or set of conditions. The questions require you to draw conclusions from the situation. Solving these questions may often require you to draw simple diagrams to sort and understand the information presented in the question.
- *Analysis of explanation.* Analysis of explanation questions appear in groups. The questions require you to assess explanations. The questions are based on a situation and its results. This question type is a recent addition to the GRE.

SKILLS TO BOOST YOUR SCORE

There are four general strategies that will better prepare you for answering analytical ability questions:

1. *Review the basics of logic.* Analytical ability questions call for you to reason logically to deduce sound conclusions from situations. If you took an introductory logic course in college, review your course materials (if you still have them).
2. *Use test prep reviews.* The Arco GRE guides listed in the Introduction to this book offer in-depth reviews of analytical questions. Sound instructional material is provided along with hundreds of practice questions

and expert test-wise strategies. For concentrated practice on analytical reasoning questions, use Arco's *GRE-LSAT Logic Workbook* (2nd ed.).

3. *Read specialized materials regularly*. This will help you strengthen your critical and analytical reading skills for logical reasoning and analysis of explanation questions.

4. *Review graphs and tables*. Reread appropriate math sections in Arco's GRE books. While any graphs or tables you get on logical reasoning sections will be easy to interpret, you don't want to lose any time figuring out how to read a graph.

Understanding Logical Reasoning Questions

Logical reasoning questions measure your understanding of an argument and your ability to recognize the structural parts of an argument. You will have to read a statement, graph, or table and draw conclusions from the evidence presented. ETS states that no specialized ability is required to answer these questions. Study the sample logical reasoning question in Figure 19.1.

> *Directions:* Each of the following questions or question groups is based upon a short passage, set of conditions, graph, or table. You might find it useful to draw a diagram to answer some of these questions. Choose the best answer choice for each question given.
>
> There are no lower non-stop coach fares between New York City and Miami, Florida than those of Global Airlines.
>
> Which of the following is logically inconsistent with the above claim?
>
> *continues*

continued

I. EconoAir has a New York City to Miami flight with a stopover in Raleigh, NC, that is priced at one-half that charged by Global.

II. Eagle Airlines charges the same coach fare for non-stop flights between New York City and Miami as Global charges.

III. SunSouth Air has a lower non-stop coach fare from New York City to Tampa than does Global.

(A) I only
(B) II only
(C) I and II only
(D) I, II, and III
(E) none of the statements is inconsistent

The answer is **(E)**. Careful reading shows that this is the only logical conclusion. First, the passage does not say that Global is the only airline offering this rate. So II is not inconsistent with the claim. III mentions a different route, so it is also not inconsistent with the claim. Finally, the fare in I is based on stopover, not non-stop, service.

Figure 19.1 Sample logical reasoning question.

Now review the following strategies.

- Read the question before reading the passage. This will help you focus your reading.
- Read the question extremely carefully and pay close attention to what information the question is asking for. Watch for thought-reversers in the question that reverse the structure of the question.
- Be prepared to dissect the argument—both its premise(s) and conclusion. Try to rephrase the argument in your own words.

UNDERSTANDING ANALYTICAL REASONING QUESTIONS

Analytical reasoning questions measure your ability to understand and to draw conclusions from a set of conditions. Each question in an analytical reasoning group is based on the same set of conditions. However, the questions are independent of one another. Study the sample analytical reasoning question in Figure 19.2.

Directions: Each of the following questions or question groups is based on a short passage, set of conditions, graph, or table. You might find it useful to draw a diagram to answer some of these questions. Choose the best answer choice for each question given.

The musical director of the community playhouse is scheduling auditions for eight singers—J, K, L, M, N, O, P, and Q—the same week as rehearsals. Each singer will have one audition and all auditions are to be held Monday through Friday of that same week.

At least one singer will be auditioned each day.

More than one audition will be scheduled on exactly two of the days.

O is the only singer who will be auditioned on Wednesday.

M and N must be scheduled for auditions exactly three days after Q.

P must be interviewed later in the week than K.

If M, N, and K are auditioned on the same day, which of the following must be true?

continues

continued

(A) J is auditioned on Monday.
(B) Q is auditioned on Monday.
(C) L is interviewed on Tuesday.
(D) J and L are interviewed on the same day.
(E) J and Q are interviewed on the same day.

For this question, **(B)** is the correct answer. First, since the auditions must be in the same week and M and N can only be auditioned three days after Q, then M and N can be auditioned only on Thursday or Friday. Second, since P must follow later in the week than K and K must be auditioned on the same day as M and N, then M and N can only be scheduled for Thursday. This requires that Q be auditioned on Monday.

Figure 19.2 Sample analytical reasoning question.

Now review the following strategies.

- Take time to read each question carefully and understand all the conditions. If you need to set up a diagram, make it clear and understandable.
- Do not be intimidated by seemingly complicated problems. Use your own shorthand to summarize information for easy reference.
- If necessary, underline or circle important terms and conditions in the test booklet.
- Do not look for hidden meanings in a problem or read extraneous assumptions in a condition.

SUMMARY

In this lesson you learned skills and strategies for solving two analytical reasoning question types—logical reasoning and analytical reasoning.

LESSON 20

Preparing for the Analytical Sections—Part 2

In this lesson you will learn about the third question type tested on GRE analytical ability sections—analysis of explanations.

Understanding Analysis of Explanation Questions

Analysis of explanation questions measure your ability to understand causal explanations for situations and their results. Analysis of explanation questions are grouped in sets consisting of (1) situation, (2) result, and (3) questions followed by numbered statements.

> **!** **Don't Be Intimidated** Your big challenge is not to be intimidated by the unfamiliar directions and the analysis of explanation questions. The questions are easier than they look.

Since this is a fairly recent question type, even ETS has not fully settled on its final format. However, when answering analysis of explanation questions, read each question component separately in the order the component appears in the question.

Here are the components in the current format:

> *Directions.* Be certain to read the directions quickly. The important thing to note is how many different answer choices are called for.
>
> *Situation.* The situation is a short passage about 100 words in length.
>
> *Result.* The result is the outcome of the situation.
>
> *Additional Directions with Definitions.* ETS currently provides directions that define what the questions ask for.
>
> *Questions and Numbered Statements.* There will be two questions. Each question will be followed by a series of statements. One question will ask about an "adequate explanation," the other about "relevance." The current way questions are worded is confusing. Basically, the questions ask you to (1) assume the statements are true, and (2) relate the statements to the result.

Figure 20.1 Analysis of explanations format.

UNDERSTAND DIRECTIONS

The advice for every GRE question type applies to analysis of explanation questions as well. The questions may be presented in one of three different formats:

1. Two choices (A, B) are available for each answer.
2. Three choices (A, B, C) are available for each answer.
3. Four choices (A, B, C, D) are available for each answer.

However, the overall directions are the same for each format. Read through the directions quickly and underline the directions for selecting answer choices to ensure you answer the question correctly.

Since ETS uses the two-choice format to illustrate the question, this format is followed in Figure 20.2 below.

Directions: Before each group of numbered statements is a question that can be answered either "Yes" or "No." Answer this question separately for each statement in the group by choosing answer choice "A" for "Yes" or answer choice "B" for "No" and marking the appropriate space on your answer sheet. Do not select answer choices C, D, or E for any question. Do not assume that there are more "Yes" or "No" answers in a set.

Situation: Over the past ten years, the population of Allen County has more than doubled. This increase in population has led to overcrowding at Peabody School. As a result, at the beginning of the most recent school year, 15 grammar school, 20 middle school, and 25 high school students were reassigned to Warren School, which has a larger building. Warren has seven more teachers than Peabody, but the average number of years of experience of the teachers is approximately equal for the two school systems. Both systems administer standardized achievement tests to all students at the end of each school year.

Result: At the end of the school year following the reassignment, scores achieved on the year-end achievement tests by Warren students were approximately 8 percent higher than those of the previous year.

continues

continued

The above result requires explanation. You are not to consider unlikely or farfetched explanations in the questions.

When considering statement relevance, a statement is relevant if it provides information that either supports or weakens the explanation.

Question 1: Assume that the following statement is true. Could the statement provide the basis for an adequate explanation of the result of the situation?

Statement: A new computer learning lab opened by Warren School at the beginning of the school year helped to improve the verbal and math skills of Warren students.

Question 2: Assume that the following statement is true. Is the statement relevant to a possible adequate explanation of the result of the situation?

Statement: The dramatic growth in the population of Allen County can be explained by a rapid increase in the number of employers in the area that use advanced technology.

For question 1, the answer is (**A**). The statement provides a possible explanation for the result: The computerized learning lab helped to boost scores.

For question 2, the answer is (**B**). The statement is not relevant; events that occurred ten years earlier cannot possibly explain the result of the situation.

Figure 20.2 Sample analysis of explanations question set.*

**Analysis of explanation question reprinted from* Preparation for the GRE *by Thomas H. Martinson (Arco Books, Macmillan). Reprinted with permission of the publisher.*

The following list provides question answering strategies:

- Read the situation and result carefully—anticipate explanations.
- Answer the question you feel most comfortable with first.
- Remember that negative information can be relevant. Statements that weaken a possible explanation can therefore be considered relevant.
- Do not bring information from one statement to another. Answer each statement separately.

SUMMARY

In this lesson you learned skills and strategies for solving GRE analysis of explanations questions.

LESSON 21

TAKING OTHER STANDARDIZED TESTS

In this lesson you will learn about other standardized examinations you may be required to take for graduate school admissions, including GRE Subject Tests, the Miller Analogies Test (MAT), and the Test of English as a Foreign Language (TOEFL).

GRE SUBJECT TESTS

You may be required to take one or more GRE Subject Tests in addition to the GRE General Test. Each school and program has its own requirements, so check with the graduate school admissions office as soon as possible.

Information for the Subject Tests can be obtained from Educational Testing Service at the phone number and address listed in Lesson 15. Currently, ETS is giving Subject Tests in 16 different areas:

- Biochemistry, cell and molecular biology
- Biology
- Chemistry
- Computer science
- Economics
- Revised education

- Engineering
- Geology
- History
- Literature in English
- Mathematics
- Music
- Physics
- Political science
- Psychology
- Sociology

REVIEWING FOR YOUR SUBJECT TESTS

The Subject Tests are a measure of your achievement in a subject. They test broad knowledge approximating the level of an introductory college course. Find out how much importance is given to GRE Subject Test scores by the school or department. Then take a look at a previous GRE Subject Test to see what areas of knowledge are questioned most on the test.

In addition to GRE General Test practice books, ETS also offers subject test reviews. To obtain more information, see the address and phone number given in Lesson 15.

> **!** **Know the Test Format and Beware of the Scoring Penalty** Each test is unique in length and format. All questions are multiple choice, except for some items on the music test. For Subject Tests, there is a scoring penalty: You will lose one-quarter of a point for all incorrect answers. Your raw score is converted into a scaled score ranging from 200 to 900. This procedure eliminates any advantage that may be gained through random guessing; however, an educated guess raises the odds in your favor and should be tried.

If you feel you are quite strong in a subject, you may not need to do much preparation. However, if you have been out of school for some time or require a refresher for any reason, you should:

- Buy good introductory subject or course reviews for study
- Review your college textbooks
- Review your college class notes if you have them

Table 21.1 shows recent average GRE Subject Test scores by subject.

Table 21.1 Recent GRE Average Subject Test Scores*

Year	Biology	Chemistry	Education	Engineering	Literature	Psychology
1988	615	631	467	622	525	537
1989	612	642	465	626	528	538
1990	612	662	461	617	523	537
1991	609	660	457	611	523	535
1992	605	654	462	610	525	536

**Source: Digest of Education Statistics, 1994*

Don't Overextend Yourself The Subject Tests are only offered in pencil-and-paper format. They are given in the afternoon on the same dates as the General Test. You may want to schedule the exams separately, depending on the amount of review you need.

Miller Analogies Test (MAT)

Many graduate psychology departments require the Miller Analogies Test (MAT). The MAT is not administered on a uniform date nationwide. Each test center determines its own schedule and establishes its own testing fees. To obtain a listing of test centers and an information bulletin, you should write to

Miller Analogies Test Coordinator
The Psychological Corporation
555 Academic Court
San Antonio, TX 78204-3956
Tel: 210-921-8801 or 800-622-3231

tip

Practice for Better Results While the MAT is considered an aptitude test, you will need strong vocabulary skills plus a firm grounding in literature, social studies, math, and science to do well on it. You will have 50 minutes to answer 100 analogy questions. Questions are arranged in order of difficulty and there is no penalty for guessing. Extensive practice in MAT questions is probably your best test preparation strategy.

Test of English as a Foreign Language (TOEFL) and Other Tests of English-Language Proficiency

Schools will generally require all international non-native English-speaking students to demonstrate their English language proficiency by taking a standardized test. The Test of

English as a Foreign Language (TOEFL) is the most widely used exam. Other tests that may be required are the Test of Spoken English (TSE) and the Test of Written English (TWE). All three tests are offered by Educational Testing Service. For more information, write

TOEFL, TSE, or TWE
P.O. Box 6151
Princeton, NJ 08541-6151

tip

Attain English Proficiency If you are a foreign student seeking a research or teaching assistantship, you will probably have to meet higher English proficiency standards set by individual departments to be considered for the award. Higher Test of English as a Foreign Language scores will be asked for, as well as other English proficiency tests. The Test of Spoken English (TSE) is often required in addition to the TOEFL.

REVIEWING FOR THE TESTS

For specific Arco books on the Miller Analogies Test and the Test of English as a Foreign Language, see the Introduction to this book. Studies have shown that practicing on sample tests can help boost your actual test scores.

SUMMARY

In this lesson you learned about other tests required for graduate school admissions, including the GRE Subject Tests, the Miller Analogies Test, and the Test of English as a Foreign Language.

APPENDIX A
SAMPLE APPLICATION FOR ADMISSION

Columbia GRADUATE SCHOOL OF ARTS AND SCIENCES

APPLICATION FOR ADMISSION

☐ AUTUMN TERM 19____ ☐ SPRING TERM 19____

Please type or print legibly in ink. Submit completed application with nonrefundable fee of $60 (check or money order) to 107 Low Memorial Library, Columbia University, New York, NY 10027. *If you are applying to Anatomy and Cell Biology, Biochemistry and Molecular Biophysics, Genetics and Development, Integrated Program in Cellular, Molecular, and Biophysical Studies, Medical Informatics, Microbiology, Neurobiology and Behavior, Nutrition, Pathology, Pharmacology, or Physiology and Cellular Biophysics please submit completed application to Office of Graduate Affairs, Room 406, 701 West 168th Street, New York, NY 10032.*

Proposed Department or Doctoral Program Subcommittee (select only one of the indicated programs of study)

____

Subfield______________ Regional Institute (if applicable)______________

Degree(s) desired: M.A./M.Phil./Ph.D. ☐ M.Phil./Ph.D. ☐ M.A. only (Full-Time) ☐ M.A. only (Part-Time) ☐ D.M.A. ☐

______________________________ Sex: ☐ M ☐ F

Last (family) name First name Middle name

______________ ______________

Social Security Number Please indicate above any variations of your name used on official records

Permanent address Current address Until______________

______________ ______________

______________ ______________

______________ ______________

Telephone: ______________ Telephone: ______________

Fax: ______________ Fax: ______________

Date of birth____________ (mo./day/yr.) City and country of birth ____________ e-mail: ____________

Citizenship: ☐ U.S. ☐ U.S. Permanent Resident ☐ Foreign: __________ country __________ visa type ☐ held ☐ desired

Previous education: Name and location of colleges, graduate, and professional schools, including Columbia	Dates of attendance	Degree	Date received or expected

Undergraduate major____________ Graduate ____________

Do not write below this line

☐ **Application complete** ☐ **Credentials missing**	**Department's Recommendations and Comments:** ☐ **Admit with Fellowship** ☐ **Admit** ☐ **Admit M.A. only** ☐ **Reject**	**Institute's Recommendations and Comments:** ☐ **Admit** ☐ **Reject**
For Admissions ____ *Date*	*For the Department* ____ *Date*	*For the Institute* ____ *Date*

continued

continued

Test Date		General (Aptitude)						Subject (Advanced)		
Month	Year	Verbal	%	Quant.	%	Anal.	%	Code	Score	%

Test Date: Month_______ Year_____			
Section 1	Section 2	Section 3	TOTAL

Date requested from ETS: ______________________________

OFFICAL TEST SCORES MUST ALSO BE REQUESTED FROM ETS

Please provide the following information for those individuals from whom you have requested letters of evaluation.

Full name	Title/Position and department	Institution or address	Date requested

Have you ever been dismissed or suspended from an academic institution? Yes_____ No_____
(If yes, explain fully in your Personal Statement.)

From which languages can you translate scholarly material into English? ______________________________
If proficiency was acquired by means other than course work, please describe: ______________________________

____

What academic honors have you received (e.g., prizes, scholarships, fellowships, honor societies?)

____

Academic and/or relevant work experience:

Employer	Position	Dates	Type of Work

Have you ever applied to any division of Columbia before? ____________

If so, when and which division(s)? ____________

Are you currently applying to any other division of Cclumbia? ____________

If so, which division? ____________

Are you applying for a joint degree program? ____________ If so, which? ____________

If you have discussed your application with a member of the Columbia faculty or staff, please give name and date:

____

Optional: Please list any schools other than Columbia to which you may be applying.

____

I certify that the information given by me on this application (including all supplementary pages) is complete and accurate.
I understand that failure to disclose correct information may result in the cancellation of my application or admission.

____________ ____________

Signature Date

Appendix B
Sample Personal Statement Form

Columbia

GRADUATE SCHOOL OF ARTS AND SCIENCES

PERSONAL STATEMENT

In a statement of approximately 500 words, describe your background, your past work in your intended field of study, and your plans for graduate study and a professional career. If you are currently in a graduate program at another university, please explain why you wish to leave. If you are not currently enrolled in an academic program, please describe your activities since last registered. Please typewrite or word-process. Return this form with your application.

Last (family) name ____________ First name ____________ Middle name ____________

Date of birth ____________ Social Security Number ____________

Proposed department or program ____________

(Please use both sides of form if necessary.)

Reprinted with permission from Columbia University, Graduate School of Arts and Sciences.

APPENDIX C
SAMPLE LETTER OF EVALUATION FORM

Columbia

GRADUATE SCHOOL OF ARTS AND SCIENCES

LETTER OF EVALUATION

A. To the Applicant: Please give one of these forms to each of the three academic sponsors you select, along with an envelope marked "Evaluation Letter." Ask the sponsor to seal the letter he or she has written on your behalf in the envelope, sign across the seal, and return it to you. Do not open this envelope or break the seal. Submit the sealed envelopes containing your letters of evaluation with your application package. If you have been away from an academic institution for some time, this form may be given to some other person who is able to comment on your academic qualifications.

____

Last (family) name First name Middle name

______________________ ______________________

Date of birth Social Security Number

Proposed department or program ______________________

Name of academic sponsor ______________________

Under the Family Educational Rights and Privacy Act of 1974 (Buckley Amendment), which gives registered students the right to inspect and review their educational records, students may waive their right to see specific confidential statements and letters of evaluation. In the belief that applicants, and the persons from whom they request evaluations, may wish to preserve the confidentiality of those evaluations, we are giving you an opportunity to sign one of the following statements:

(1) I waive my right to examine this letter.

Please check ☐ ______________________
(your signature)

(2) I do not waive my right to examine this letter.

Please check ☐ ______________________
(your signature)

- -

B. To the Academic Sponsor: This form is submitted to you for an opinion of the applicant's qualifications for graduate work. If possible, please compare the student with others known to you who have attended or are now applying for admission to this school. If the applicant requesting this evaluation has signed statement (2) or has signed neither of the statements above, this letter will be available for the applicant's examination should he or she enroll in the Graduate School. This evaluation is to be mailed or given to the applicant in the envelope provided. Please seal and sign the back flap of the envelope; the letter will be submitted unopened by the applicant with his or her application.

Please check if this letter may not be used by the Graduate School for fellowship competitions and similar purposes if the student registers ☐

SIGNATURE ______________________ NAME (print) ______________________

TITLE ______________________ INSTITUTION ______________________ DATE ____________

(please use both sides of form if necessary)

INDEX

A

Appendix C
Sample Letter of Evaluation Form

Columbia GRADUATE SCHOOL OF ARTS AND SCIENCES

LETTER OF EVALUATION

A. To the Applicant: Please give one of these forms to each of the three academic sponsors you select, along with an envelope marked "Evaluation Letter." Ask the sponsor to seal the letter he or she has written on your behalf in the envelope, sign across the seal, and return it to you. Do not open this envelope or break the seal. Submit the sealed envelopes containing your letters of evaluation with your application package. If you have been away from an academic institution for some time, this form may be given to some other person who is able to comment on your academic qualifications.

Last (family) name ______ First name ______ Middle name ______

Date of birth ______ Social Security Number ______

Proposed department or program ______

Name of academic sponsor ______

Under the Family Educational Rights and Privacy Act of 1974 (Buckley Amendment), which gives registered students the right to inspect and review their educational records, students may waive their right to see specific confidential statements and letters of evaluation. In the belief that applicants, and the persons from whom they request evaluations, may wish to preserve the confidentiality of those evaluations, we are giving you an opportunity to sign one of the following statements:

(1) I waive my right to examine this letter.

Please check ☐ ______ (your signature)

(2) I do not waive my right to examine this letter.

Please check ☐ ______ (your signature)

B. To the Academic Sponsor: This form is submitted to you for an opinion of the applicant's qualifications for graduate work. If possible, please compare the student with others known to you who have attended or are now applying for admission to this school. If the applicant requesting this evaluation has signed statement (2) or has signed neither of the statements above, this letter will be available for the applicant's examination should he or she enroll in the Graduate School. This evaluation is to be mailed or given to the applicant in the envelope provided. Please seal and sign the back flap of the envelope; the letter will be submitted unopened by the applicant with his or her application.

Please check if this letter may not be used by the Graduate School for fellowship competitions and similar purposes if the student registers ☐

SIGNATURE ______ NAME (print) ______

TITLE ______ INSTITUTION ______ DATE ______

(please use both sides of form if necessary)

Index

A

G–H

I

J–K

L

M

N

O

P

Q